Grief and Loss Moving Forward with Love

By Jiles Smith II and Dr. Sheila Mallett-Smith

Published by Isham Media Group LLC

This book is for educational purposes. It is not legal, medical, or clinical advice. Readers should consult qualified professionals for guidance specific to their situation.

ISBN 978-1-967055-21-0

TABLE OF CONTENTS

Our Journey Through Loss and Love

Grief entered our lives in different seasons and under different circumstances. Before our paths joined, each of us endured losses that reshaped our lives. What follows are personal reflections on those experiences, not to define grief for others, but to acknowledge the paths that brought us to this work.

We did not live the same losses, but over time, we have come to understand one another's grief with respect, patience, and care.

Jiles' Journey

Grief entered my life in a way I could not have anticipated. I lost my daughter, Ursula Martin Smith, at twenty-five years old. She was struck by a driver under the influence, a sudden loss that altered the direction of my life in ways I am still learning to understand.

Ursula was not only my daughter; she was someone I deeply admired. Track and field connected us. In high school, she became the state 400-meter champion, but what stays with me most is her discipline and steadiness. We spoke often about track and field, especially the curve, the part of the track where focus and strength matter most, when the finish line is not yet visible. At the time, it was simply something we shared. Later, I would realize how much that image reflected my own journey through grief.

Years later, I lost my son, Dr. Lamar J. Smith, at thirty-three due to medical complications. Losing one child changes the way you see the world. Losing two reshapes the way you move through it. There are moments when that reality feels heavy, and others when it settles quietly in the background of daily life. People often say parents are not meant to outlive their children. While that may be true in principle, life does not always unfold according to what feels natural or fair.

Grief did not follow a straight line. It moved in and out of my days. Some seasons carried intense sorrow; others held quieter moments of reflection and memory. Over time I began to understand that I was not being asked to leave my children behind, but to carry them differently. Love does not disappear when someone is gone. It changes form, but it remains.

Many people loved Ursula and Lamar, and each carries a different story of loss. Their grief belongs to them. I share only my experience as their father, from the place their lives occupied in my own.

Sheila's Journey

My journey through grief unfolded differently. I was married to my husband for twenty-six years, defined less by anniversaries than by the life we slowly built together. Evenings talking long after the day was done, projects around the house, time spent working in the yard, traditions that formed quietly over time, and the steady comfort of knowing someone had walked beside you through most of your adult life. We built a home shaped by ordinary days as much as by milestone moments. The future did not feel uncertain; it felt assumed.

When he was diagnosed with cancer, our lives shifted into a different rhythm. The loss did not arrive suddenly. It unfolded over two years of treatments, appointments, research, and difficult decisions. As a nurse, I approached the illness the way I had approached many challenges in my professional life: by advocating, asking questions, seeking second opinions, consulting specialists, and challenging insurance decisions when necessary. I moved between hospital rooms and medical journals, between hope and realism. I believed that if I worked hard enough and stayed vigilant enough, we could outmaneuver the disease.

When we lost him, grief carried more than absence. It carried exhaustion, and the quiet question many caregivers know too well: Did I miss something? Could I have done more? Even with everything we tried, I had to face the reality that love and effort are not always enough to change an outcome.

Our life together included my two daughters, his two daughters, and our grandchildren—family, however layered, gathered around the same table over the years.

When he died, that rhythm stopped.

The loss was not only of the man I loved; it was the interruption of a long partnership. After twenty-six years, understanding lives in small things such as a glance across a room, the familiarity of someone's presence, and the comfort of being known without explanation. His absence appeared in unexpected ways: paperwork that needed attention, holidays that felt different, quiet moments at the end of the day.

Each member of our family experienced that loss in her own way. Their grief belongs to them. I speak only from the place I occupied, as a wife who fought beside her husband for as long as she could and then had to learn how to live without him.

Over time, I learned that healing does not erase what was. Continuing forward does not cancel the past. Love does not diminish when life expands. It becomes part of the foundation that steadies you.

My grief did not disappear when I began rebuilding my life. It changed shape. What we built together remains part of me, not as something replaced, but as something foundational.

Reflection on Grief

Grief has taught us that loss is never one-size-fits-all, because love is never one-size-fits-all. Each relationship carries its own language, memories, and shared experiences. When that person is gone, the absence touches every corner of life in ways that are both visible and deeply personal.

Sometimes loss arrives suddenly, leaving the mind struggling to understand what has happened. Other times it unfolds slowly through illness and caregiving, where hope and fear exist side by side. However it comes, grief reshapes daily life—the calendar, the home, and the way we imagine the future.

Grief is rarely a single emotion. It can include sorrow, anger, gratitude, regret, numbness, and longing, sometimes all within the same day. Two people can experience the same loss and still carry entirely different grief, because each bond is unique.

Moving forward does not mean leaving someone behind. It means learning how to carry love differently. Over time, many people discover that grief does not disappear; it becomes woven into the larger story of who they are and how they continue living.

Introduction: Navigating the Landscape of Grief and Loss

Grief is a universal experience, yet it is also one of the most deeply personal journeys we will ever undertake. It is the natural response to the loss of someone or something that mattered deeply. When loss enters our lives, the world can feel unfamiliar. The routines and expectations that once felt stable may suddenly seem uncertain.

Grief rarely unfolds in predictable ways. It is shaped by our relationships, our histories, the circumstances surrounding the loss, and the support systems available to us. What comforts one person may not help another. What feels manageable one day may feel overwhelming the next.

This book is intended as a companion for those navigating the landscape of grief and loss. It does not offer a formula for healing or a timetable for recovery. Instead, it provides perspective, practical tools, and reflections that acknowledge the many ways people experience grief.

Whether you are grieving the death of a loved one, supporting someone who is, or simply seeking a deeper understanding of loss, this book was written with you in mind.

The Purpose of This Book

Grief is often misunderstood. In many cultures, there is pressure to move past loss quickly or to return to normal as soon as possible. But grief is not a problem to solve or a stage of life to complete. It is a process that unfolds over time.

The purpose of this book is to explore the many dimensions of grief and offer guidance to those learning to live with loss. The chapters that follow are organized into four parts, each addressing a different aspect of the grieving experience.

Understanding Grief: This section explores the nature of grief, its stages, and its many forms. It delves into the emotional, physical, and psychological dimensions of loss, helping you make sense of the often-overwhelming feelings that accompany it.

Navigating the Pain: Here, we examine the challenges of living with grief, from the isolation it can bring to the struggle of finding meaning in the midst of pain. This section offers practical tools and strategies for coping with the day-to-day realities of loss.

Finding Light in the Darkness: In this part, we explore the ways grief can lead to growth and transformation. From honoring the legacy of a loved one to finding joy and purpose again, these chapters offer hope and inspiration for those seeking to rebuild their lives.

Moving Forward with Love: The final section focuses on the journey of healing and renewal. It addresses the role of forgiveness, the impact of grief on relationships, and the power of rituals and storytelling in keeping a loved one's memory alive.

A Note on Grief's Uniqueness

No two grief journeys are the same. Your experience of loss is shaped by your relationship with the person who has died, the circumstances of their death, your personality, your cultural background, and countless other factors. What helps one person may not help another, and that is okay. This book is not meant to prescribe a "right" way to grieve. Instead, it offers a range of perspectives and tools, inviting you to take what resonates and leave what does not.

The Role of Stories

Throughout this book, you will find personal and universal stories that illustrate the many faces of grief. These stories are not meant to provide formulas for healing but to offer connection and understanding. They remind us that we are not alone in our pain and that others have walked this path before us. Stories have the power to comfort, to inspire, and to remind us of our shared humanity.

A Journey of Love and Loss

At its core, grief is an expression of love. It is the shadow cast by a bond that matters deeply. To grieve is to acknowledge that love does not end when a life ends. Instead, it continues to change form as we learn to carry memory, meaning, and connection forward.

This book is an invitation to honor that love: to hold it close, carry it forward, and discover how it can continue to shape your life even after loss.

As you read these pages, we hope you will find understanding, compassion, and perhaps moments of hope. Grief can feel like a heavy burden, but it is one we do not have to carry alone. Together we can learn to navigate the pain, find light in the darkness, and move forward with love.

With compassion and solidarity,

Jiles Smith II and Sheila Mallett-Smith

Part 1: The Weight of Loss

Chapter 1

The Moment Everything Changed

Processing the Initial Shock of Loss

The moment loss enters our lives, the world can feel unfamiliar. Time slows, ordinary routines lose their meaning, and reality becomes difficult to grasp. In those first moments, we are simply trying to understand what has happened.

The Fog of Grief

How the Mind and Body React to Sudden Loss

Grief is an inevitable part of the human experience, yet its arrival often feels like an uninvited storm that leaves devastation in its wake. The initial shock of loss is often described as a fog that settles over the mind and body, obscuring clarity and distorting reality. This fog is not only a metaphor; it reflects the physiological and psychological response to the sudden absence of someone deeply significant.

When loss occurs, the brain is often the first to react. The amygdala, the part of the brain responsible for processing emotions, becomes highly active, triggering a surge of stress hormones such as cortisol and adrenaline (O'Connor, 2019). This hormonal surge can lead to a range of physical symptoms, including nausea, dizziness, and a racing heart. The prefrontal cortex, which governs rational thought and decision-making, becomes impaired, making it difficult to think clearly or make sense of the situation (Shear, 2015). The resulting disorientation is why many people describe the early experience of grief as moving through a mental fog.

The body, too, responds to loss in profound ways. Grief can manifest as physical pain, fatigue, and even a weakened immune system (Stroebe, Schut, & Stroebe, 2007). The stress of loss can disrupt sleep patterns, leading to insomnia or excessive sleeping. Appetite may vanish, or conversely, one may find solace in food. These physical reactions are not merely side effects; they are integral to the grieving process, signaling the body's attempt to cope with an overwhelming emotional burden.

The fog of grief also affects a person's perception of time. Minutes can feel like hours, and days may blur together in a haze of sorrow. This distortion of time is common after a sudden loss, as the mind struggles to reconcile the past with the present (Neimeyer, 2016). The world may appear to continue as usual, yet for the grieving individual, time often feels suspended in disbelief.

Within this fog, emotions can shift quickly and unpredictably. Anger, guilt, sadness, and even moments of relief may surface in rapid succession. These emotions are not mutually exclusive; they often coexist, creating a complicated emotional landscape that can be difficult to navigate. The grieving person may feel overwhelmed by their intensity, unsure how to process what they are experiencing or where to turn for support.

The fog of grief is not a sign of weakness or failure. It reflects the mind and body's natural response to profound loss. In many ways, this mental and emotional haze acts as a form of protection, allowing the individual to absorb the reality of the loss gradually. Although the fog can feel suffocating, it also serves as a temporary buffer against the full force of grief.

The First 24 Hours

Navigating the Immediate Aftermath

The first 24 hours after a loss are often the most disorienting and emotionally charged. During this initial period, the grieving person is thrust into a whirlwind of practical concerns and emotional turmoil. The shock is still fresh, and the mind struggles to comprehend the magnitude of what has happened.

During this time, reactions can vary widely from numbness to overwhelming emotion. Some individuals experience disbelief, unable to accept that the loss has occurred. Others may feel flooded with emotion, cry uncontrollably, or react with anger. These responses are normal and reflect the mind's effort to absorb the enormity of the loss.

Practical concerns often take center stage in the first 24 hours. Arrangements must be made, people notified, and decisions reached. For many, these tasks feel surreal, as if they are happening to someone else. The grieving person may feel detached from their own actions, moving through responsibilities without fully engaging with the reality of the situation.

Support from friends and family can be invaluable during this time, yet it may also feel overwhelming. Well-meaning loved ones offer condolences, advice, or help, but their presence can sometimes feel intrusive to someone still in shock. The grieving person may struggle to communicate what they need or feel guilty for not expressing gratitude for the support being offered.

The first 24 hours are also a time of heightened vulnerability. Grieving individuals may feel exposed, as if their emotions are visible to everyone around them. Some worry about how they are perceived or fear they are not grieving "correctly." These concerns are common but can add another layer of stress to an already painful moment.

Amid the chaos of those early hours, it helps to remember that there is no single "right" way to grieve. Every loss is experienced differently, shaped by the relationship we had, the circumstances surrounding the death, and our own emotional makeup. Grief does not follow a schedule. The first twenty-four hours are only the beginning of a long and often difficult road. In those early moments, the kindest thing we can offer ourselves is patience and gentleness.

The Phone Call

One woman described the moment she learned her husband had died in a car accident as the moment the world divided into two versions of time: before the call and after it.

The voice on the other end of the line sounded calm, almost rehearsed. At first, she assumed there had been a mistake. People do not simply disappear from ordinary life in the middle of a Tuesday afternoon. She asked the same question more than once, hoping the answer might somehow change.

Later, she would remember small details with surprising clarity—the clock on the wall, the hum of the refrigerator, the strange quiet of the house. Yet the meaning of the words took much longer to settle in.

In those first moments, grief often arrives not as an overwhelming emotion but as disbelief. The mind struggles to absorb a reality it was never prepared to face.

When Reality Sets In

The Slow Realization of Permanence

As the initial shock subsides, the grieving person is often confronted with the slow, painful realization of permanence. Loss is no longer an abstract concept; it is a concrete reality that must be faced. This realization can be one of the most difficult aspects of grief, as it requires the individual to come to terms with the fact that their loved one is gone and will not return.

This phase is often marked by deep sadness and longing. The grieving person may replay memories of their loved one, searching the past for comfort. Many also experience profound emptiness, as if a part of themselves has been permanently altered. This feeling can be especially intense after the loss of a spouse or partner, when the absence of a life companion leaves a space that feels impossible to fill.

The realization of permanence can also bring growing isolation. Grieving individuals may feel that no one else truly understands their pain, leading to loneliness and withdrawal. Social interactions can become difficult, particularly with people who have not experienced a similar loss. Well-intentioned attempts at comfort—such as suggestions to "move on" or "find closure"—can unintentionally deepen this sense of isolation.

During this period, many people begin to wrestle with deeper questions about life, death, and meaning, as individuals attempt to reconstruct a sense of purpose and coherence after loss (Neimeyer, 2012). Loss can shake long-held beliefs or challenge a person's faith. Questions arise about why the loss occurred, whether suffering has purpose, and what the future might look like without the person who has died. These questions are a natural part of grief and reflect how deeply loss reshapes a person's understanding of the world.

The gradual realization of permanence is painful but necessary. It is a period of reflection as the grieving person begins to rebuild life in the absence of their loved one. While the pain of loss may never disappear entirely, it often becomes more manageable over time, allowing space for new meaning and renewed purpose.

Chapter Exercise: Finding Ground in the First 24 Hours

Purpose:

This exercise helps you acknowledge the shock of loss and begin grounding yourself when reality feels overwhelming. It's designed to bring gentle awareness to your body and surroundings when emotions feel disoriented.

Step 1 – Remember the Moment

Take a quiet moment and write about when you first realized your loved one was gone. Don't worry about structure, just describe what you remember: the sights, sounds, sensations, or thoughts that came up.

Prompt:

What do you remember about that moment? What felt most real, and what felt like a blur?

Step 2 – Identify What You Felt in Your Body

Grief often begins as a physical reaction before it becomes emotional.

Write down how your body responded in those early hours—tightness, shaking, numbness, exhaustion, or anything else.

Prompt:

How did your body react to the news? Where did you feel the loss physically?

Step 3 – Anchor in the Present

Now, practice a short grounding technique.

Look around and name 5 things you can see

4 things you can touch

3 things you can hear

2 things you can smell

1 thing you can taste or imagine tasting

This helps bring your mind back to safety and presence when waves of shock return.

Step 4 – Write a Note of Self-Compassion

Write a brief note to yourself as if you were comforting a close friend going through the same loss.

Prompt:

What would you say to someone you care about who is experiencing this? What would you want them to remember about surviving the first moments of loss?

Keep this note somewhere visible—a reminder that you are surviving something profoundly hard, one breath at a time.

References

Neimeyer, R. A. (2012). Techniques of grief therapy: Creative practices for counseling the bereaved. Routledge.

Neimeyer, R. A. (2016). Techniques of grief therapy: Assessment and intervention. Routledge.

O'Connor, M.-F. (2019). Grief: A brief history of research on how body, mind, and brain adapt. Psychosomatic Medicine, 81(8), 731–738.

Shear, M. K. (2015). Complicated grief treatment: The theory, practice, and outcomes. Depression and Anxiety, 32(8), 553–560.

Stroebe, M., Schut, H., & Stroebe, W. (2007). Health outcomes of bereavement. The Lancet, 370(9603), 1960–1973.

Chapter 2

Grief Has No Timeline

Understanding That Healing Is Not Linear

Grief rarely follows the schedules we expect. Some days bring calm, while others reopen the pain without warning. Healing does not move in straight lines; it unfolds slowly, in its own time.

The Myth of "Getting Over It"

Why Grief Doesn't Have an Expiration Date

One of the most pervasive myths about grief is that it is something to be "gotten over." This notion suggests that grief is a finite process with a clear endpoint, after which the grieving person can return to their normal life. However, this could not be further from the truth. Grief rarely unfolds in a straight line with a clear beginning, middle, and end. Instead, it evolves over time and often remains a part of life in ways that change but never fully disappear.

The idea of "getting over" grief reflects a broader cultural discomfort with prolonged sadness and vulnerability. Society often expects individuals to "move on" after a certain period, as if grief were a task to complete rather than a journey to navigate. These expectations can be harmful, placing pressure on grieving individuals to conform to an arbitrary timeline (Worden, 2018).

Living with loss often involves gradual adaptation. People begin to find ways to carry the absence of someone they love while continuing with the responsibilities and rhythms of daily life. Remembering and moving forward can coexist, allowing memory, love, and loss to become part of the larger story of a life. Grief scholars describe this adjustment as part of the ongoing process of integrating loss into one's life narrative (Neimeyer, 2016).

The myth of "getting over" grief can also create guilt and self-doubt. Grieving individuals may feel they are not progressing quickly enough or that something is wrong if sadness and longing continue. These feelings are often intensified by well-meaning but misguided comments from others, such as "It's time to move on" or "You should be over it by now."

Grief is deeply personal, and there is no single "right" way to grieve. Each person's experience is shaped by the relationship they had with the person who died, the circumstances of the loss, their personality, and the support available to them. Rather than striving to "get over" grief, the goal is to learn how to live with it, honoring the memory of the loved one while continuing to engage with life.

The Rollercoaster of Emotions

Good Days, Bad Days, and Everything in Between

Grief is often described as a rollercoaster, filled with ups and downs, twists and turns. One day, the grieving person may feel relatively steady, able to move through daily routines with a degree of normalcy. The next day, a wave of sadness, anger, or despair may surface without warning. These emotional shifts are a natural part of grieving and reflect the complex nature of loss.

The unpredictability of grief can be one of its most difficult aspects. Just when someone believes they are beginning to regain their footing, a sudden surge of emotion may return, making it feel as though they are back at the beginning. These moments can be frustrating and discouraging, sometimes leading to feelings of hopelessness.

Such fluctuations are a normal part of the grieving process. Grief does not progress steadily from pain to healing. Instead, it moves through peaks and valleys—moments of clarity or acceptance followed by periods when the pain of loss resurfaces. Gradually, the peaks may become more frequent and the valleys less intense, but the emotional movement of grief rarely disappears entirely (Stroebe & Schut, 1999).

Emotional shifts are often influenced by reminders in everyday life. Anniversaries, holidays, and other significant dates can reopen feelings of loss. Even ordinary experiences—hearing a familiar song or seeing a place connected to a loved one—can bring memories rushing back and stir deep emotion.

During this unpredictable journey, self-compassion becomes essential. There is no single "right" way to move through grief, and difficult days are part of the process. What matters is allowing emotions to surface without judgment or self-criticism. By acknowledging the full range of feelings that grief brings, individuals can gradually find moments of balance and quiet resilience.

Triggers and Setbacks

How Unexpected Moments Can Reopen Wounds

One of the most challenging aspects of grief is how unexpected moments can reopen wounds that seemed to be healing. These triggers may arise from something as simple as a familiar scent or a passing comment, suddenly stirring emotions that catch a grieving person off guard.

Such triggers are a natural part of the grieving process because they reflect the deep connections we form with those we love. The brain links certain experiences with specific memories, and these associations can be powerful. A particular song, for example, may recall a shared moment with a loved one, bringing back emotions that had quietly lingered beneath the surface.

Although these moments can be painful, they can also support healing. When individuals allow themselves to experience the emotions that arise, they often begin to process grief more deeply. This can be difficult, as it requires confronting painful memories and feelings, but it is an important part of learning to live with loss (Neimeyer, 2016).

Another common experience in grief is the feeling of moving backward just when progress seems possible. At times, just as life begins to feel manageable, a setback may occur, bringing the pain of loss rushing back. These moments can feel discouraging, but they are a normal part of the grieving process.

Setbacks may arise from many sources, including external stress, unresolved emotions, or significant life events. The birth of a child, the beginning of a new relationship, or even a meaningful milestone can stir memories of the person who has died. These moments may awaken feelings of longing or sadness that had previously settled.

In the face of triggers and setbacks, self-compassion becomes essential. Grief is complex, and moments of vulnerability are part of the process. By treating themselves with patience and seeking support when needed, grieving individuals can continue moving forward—even when the path is uneven.

Conclusion

Grief is a deeply personal and often turbulent experience, shaped by many emotions and reactions. The initial shock of loss can create a mental fog that obscures clarity, while the gradual realization of permanence brings deep sadness and longing. Grief rarely unfolds in orderly stages. Instead, it shifts and changes over time, appearing in different ways throughout life.

The belief that grief must eventually be "gotten over" places unnecessary pressure on those who are mourning. In reality, grief is a process of adaptation. People learn to carry the loss, weaving it into their lives as they continue forward. The emotional ups and downs of grief, along with the triggers and setbacks that reopen wounds, are all part of that journey (Worden, 2018).

By acknowledging the full range of emotions and practicing self-compassion, individuals can gradually regain balance. Grief is not something to overcome or erase. It becomes something we learn to live with, honor, and integrate into the story of our lives. In time, many discover that even in the presence of loss, new meaning and purpose can emerge.

Exercise: Mapping Your Emotional Landscape

Purpose:

To help you visualize the ups and downs of your healing process, understand emotional triggers, and recognize progress even when it doesn't feel linear.

Instructions:

1. Draw a Line Graph:

On a sheet of paper, draw a simple horizontal timeline. Label the far-left side "The Day of Loss" and the far-right side "Today."

2. Plot Your Emotions:

Think back through the days, weeks, or months since your loss. Mark moments of deep sadness, days of calm, or unexpected joy as peaks and valleys on the graph.

Use high points for moments of peace, laughter, or connection.

Use low points for times of grief, loneliness, or pain.

3. Add Triggers and Milestones:

Annotate major dates or events that influenced your emotions such as birthdays, holidays, anniversaries, songs, or even random memories that stirred emotion.

4. Reflect:

What patterns do you notice?

Are there moments where you began to feel a little lighter?

How do setbacks or "bad days" fit into the bigger picture of your healing?

5. Write a Short Reflection (1–2 paragraphs):

Summarize what this timeline shows you about your healing. You may find that while grief doesn't follow a straight line, there's still movement—and that movement is growth.

Takeaway:

Healing isn't about erasing pain or reaching a finish line. It's about noticing that even through the waves, you're still moving forward.

References

Neimeyer, R. A. (2016). *Techniques of grief therapy: Assessment and intervention.* Routledge.

Stroebe, M., & Schut, H. (1999). The dual process model of coping with bereavement: Rationale and description. *Death Studies, 23*(3), 197–224.

Worden, J. W. (2018). *Grief counseling and grief therapy: A handbook for the mental health practitioner* (5th ed.). Springer Publishing Company.

Chapter 3

The Many Faces of Grief

Exploring Different Emotional Responses to Loss

Before we understood the language of grief, we simply felt its weight. Some days, the emotion was obvious: sadness, anger, exhaustion. Other days, it was harder to name. Over time, we realized that grief does not wear a single face. It appears in many forms.

Anger, Sadness, and Numbness

The Emotional Landscape of Grief

Grief is often associated with sadness, but the emotional landscape of loss is far more complex. Many people experience anger, confusion, numbness, guilt, relief, or even moments of unexpected calm. These emotions do not follow a predictable sequence. They can appear suddenly, overlap with one another, or return long after we believe we have moved past them. Researchers note that grief rarely unfolds in a uniform pattern, and emotional responses often shift as individuals adapt to the reality of loss (Worden, 2018).

Rather than viewing these emotions as problems to solve, it can be helpful to see them as signals—expressions of the mind and body as they adjust to a profound change. Grief scholars often describe bereavement as a process of psychological and emotional adaptation in which individuals gradually learn to integrate the loss into their lives (Neimeyer, 2012).

Anger: The Fire of Grief

Anger is a common response to loss, yet it is often misunderstood or stigmatized. Many grieving individuals feel guilty for experiencing anger, believing it to be inappropriate or unjustified. Anger can be a natural reaction to the pain and disruption that loss brings. Grief researchers have long recognized anger as a frequent emotional response to bereavement, particularly when individuals struggle with feelings of helplessness or injustice (Kubler-Ross & Kessler, 2005).

Anger may appear in different forms. Some people feel anger toward the person who died, especially if the death was sudden or preventable. Others direct anger toward themselves, believing they should have done something differently. Still others feel anger toward circumstances, fate, or the world itself, questioning why such a loss had to occur.

Although anger can feel overwhelming, it is not inherently destructive. When acknowledged and expressed in healthy ways, it can become a powerful force for reflection and growth. Some people channel anger into advocacy, working to prevent similar tragedies. Others use it as a catalyst for examining unresolved feelings or relationships.

When anger is ignored or suppressed, however, it may surface in harmful ways—lashing out at others or turning inward through self-destructive habits. Healthy outlets such as physical activity, creative expression, counseling, or open conversation can help release these emotions in constructive ways (Worden, 2018).

Sadness: The Heart of Grief

Sadness is perhaps the most universally recognized emotion associated with grief. It is the deep, aching sorrow that comes with the realization that someone or something cherished is gone forever. This sadness can touch every part of life, making it difficult to experience joy or meaning in everyday moments.

The sadness of grief can linger for weeks, months, or even years. It may ebb and flow, intensifying at certain moments, such as anniversaries or holidays, and receding at others. This ebb and flow is a natural part of the grieving process, reflecting the mind's attempt to process and integrate the loss (Neimeyer, 2012).

For some people, sadness appears through tears; for others, it feels like a heavy weight that settles quietly into daily life. Some individuals may feel a profound sense of emptiness, as if a part of themselves has been irrevocably lost. This emptiness can be particularly acute in the case of a spouse or partner, as the loss of a life companion can leave a void that is difficult to fill.

While sadness is a painful emotion, it is also an essential part of the healing process. By allowing themselves to fully experience their sadness, grieving individuals can begin to process their loss and find a way to move forward. Suppressing or avoiding sadness can prolong the grieving process, as it prevents the individual from confronting and working through their emotions (Worden, 2018).

Numbness: The Shield of Grief

In the early stages of grief, many individuals experience periods of numbness or emotional detachment. This numbness is not a sign of indifference or lack of care; rather, it acts as a psychological buffer that allows the mind to absorb the shock of loss gradually. Researchers note that emotional numbing often occurs during the early phases of bereavement as individuals struggle to comprehend the reality of what has happened (Parkes & Prigerson, 2010).

Numbness can manifest as a lack of emotion, a sense of unreality, or a feeling of being disconnected from the world. The grieving person may go through the motions of daily life without fully engaging with their surroundings or emotions. This detachment can be disorienting, leaving the individual feeling as though they are watching their life from a distance.

While numbness can provide temporary protection from overwhelming pain, it can become problematic if it lingers too long. Healing eventually requires reconnecting with emotion and memory.

Gentle engagement with meaningful experiences can help restore emotional connection. Listening to music, looking through photographs, sharing stories, or speaking about the person who died can slowly reopen emotional pathways and help the grieving individual reconnect with their feelings.

Grief Looks Different for Everyone

Story

When David's mother died, the reactions within his family surprised him. His sister cried openly for weeks, often talking about their mother and sharing memories with friends and relatives. David, however, felt strangely numb. He handled paperwork, coordinated the funeral arrangements, and focused on helping others.

Some relatives quietly wondered why he seemed so composed.

What they could not see was that David's grief was unfolding differently. In the quiet hours of the night, when the house was still, the weight of the loss settled in. He replayed old conversations in his mind and found himself lingering over small reminders, his mother's handwriting on an old recipe card, the sound of her favorite music.

For David, grief was not loud or outward. It appeared in quiet moments, in memories that surfaced unexpectedly.

Over time, he came to understand that grief does not follow a single emotional pattern. Some people weep openly. Others carry their sorrow more quietly. Both expressions reflect love, and neither diminishes the depth of the loss.

When Grief Feels Like Fear

Anxiety, and Uncertainty After Loss

Grief can also evoke feelings of fear and anxiety along with sadness and anger. The loss of a loved one can shatter one's sense of security, leaving the grieving person feeling vulnerable and uncertain about the future. This fear can manifest in various ways, from generalized anxiety to specific worries about one's own mortality or the well-being of others.

The Fear of the Unknown

One of the most common sources of fear in grief is the uncertainty that follows a loss. A grieving person may feel adrift, unsure of how to navigate life without the presence of the loved one. This uncertainty can be particularly intense when the loss was sudden or unexpected, leaving little time to prepare for the changes that follow.

The disruption caused by loss can challenge the frameworks people use to understand their lives. Grief scholars have observed that bereavement often requires individuals to reconstruct meaning as they attempt to integrate the loss into their personal narrative (Neimeyer, 2012). During this period of adjustment, the future may feel unclear or overwhelming.

This fear of the unknown may manifest as anxiety about how life will continue without the person who has died. Questions about practical responsibilities, emotional stability, and the ability to find purpose again can surface unexpectedly. These concerns are common responses to the profound changes that loss brings.

The Fear of Forgetting

Another common fear in grief is the fear of forgetting the loved one. Many people worry that memories will fade with time, leaving only fragments of what once felt vivid and alive. This concern can be especially strong in the early stages of grief, when the absence of the loved one is most acutely felt.

In response, people often create ways to preserve memory. They may keep photographs, write letters, collect meaningful objects, or revisit places connected to the person who died. Grief researchers describe these efforts as part of maintaining *continuing bonds*—the ongoing emotional connection that many individuals sustain with loved ones after death (Stroebe & Schut, 1999).

These acts of remembrance can offer comfort and continuity. They help the grieving person maintain a relationship with the loved one's memory while gradually learning to live within a changed reality.

The Fear of Moving On

For some, the fear of moving on can be a significant barrier to healing. The grieving person may worry that moving on means forgetting or betraying the loved one, leading to feelings of guilt or disloyalty. This fear can prevent the individual from fully engaging with life, as they may feel that doing so would diminish the significance of their loss.

Moving on does not mean forgetting or abandoning the loved one. Healing is not about erasing the past; it is about finding a way to carry the memory of the loved one while still embracing life (Worden, 2018). By reframing the concept of moving on as a way of honoring the loved one's legacy, the grieving person can begin to find a sense of peace and purpose.

The Loneliness of Grief

Feeling Isolated Even in a Crowd

One of the most profound and often overlooked aspects of grief is the sense of loneliness it can evoke. Even in the midst of friends and family, the grieving person may feel isolated and alone, as if no one else can truly understand their pain. This loneliness can be particularly acute in cases where the loss is not widely recognized or acknowledged, such as the loss of a pet or a miscarriage.

The Isolation of Grief

The loneliness of grief is not defined by physical isolation, but by the emotional distance that can grow between the grieving person and the world around them. The grieving person may feel that their pain is invisible or misunderstood, leading to a sense of alienation from others. This isolation can be compounded by the well-meaning but often misguided attempts of others to offer comfort, such as suggesting that the grieving person "move on" or "find closure."

This sense of isolation can be particularly acute in cases where the loss is stigmatized or not widely recognized. For example, individuals who have experienced a miscarriage or the loss of a pet may find that their grief is dismissed or minimized by others, leaving them feeling unsupported and alone.

The Need for Connection

Despite the loneliness of grief, connection is an essential part of the healing process. Grieving individuals need to feel seen, heard, and understood, even if their pain cannot be fully alleviated. This connection can come from friends and family, support groups, or therapists who specialize in grief.

One way to combat the loneliness of grief is to seek out others who have experienced a similar loss. Support groups, whether in-person or online, can provide a feeling of community and understanding that is difficult to find elsewhere. These groups can offer a safe space for grieving individuals to share their experiences, express their emotions, and find comfort in the knowledge that they are not alone.

Exercise: Naming the Emotion Beneath the Surface

Purpose:

To help you identify, name, and understand the wide range of emotions that come with grief—including the ones that feel confusing or contradictory.

Instructions:

1. Set the Scene:

Find a quiet place where you can sit without distractions. Take a few slow breaths and bring to mind a recent moment when your grief felt strong—this could be a memory, a conversation, or even a quiet moment alone.

2. List Your Emotions:

Write down every feeling that comes up, even if they seem to contradict each other. Examples might include:

Anger at being left behind

Relief that a loved one's suffering ended

Guilt for not "feeling enough"

Numbness or confusion

Gratitude for the time you had together

3. Ask "What's Beneath That?"

For each emotion, ask yourself:

What is this emotion trying to tell me?

Is there another feeling underneath it?

Example: "I feel angry." → What's beneath that? "I feel scared to live without them."

4. Sort and Reflect:

Group similar emotions together (fear, sadness, love, guilt, relief). Then, write a few sentences describing what these groups reveal about your experience of grief.

5. Optional – Creative Step:

Choose one of these emotions and express it in another form—draw it, write a short poem, or describe it as a color, texture, or sound.

Reflection Questions:

Which emotions surprised you?

Are there feelings you've been avoiding or judging yourself for?

What does this tell you about the way you grieve?

Takeaway:

Grief wears many faces. Some emotions shout; others whisper. By naming them, you give each a place at the table—and in doing so, begin to understand your own healing story more deeply.

References

Kubler-Ross, E., & Kessler, D. (2005). On grief and grieving: Finding the meaning of grief through the five stages of loss. Scribner.

Neimeyer, R. A. (2012). Techniques of grief therapy: Creative practices for counseling the bereaved. Routledge.

Parkes, C. M., & Prigerson, H. G. (2010). Bereavement: Studies of grief in adult life (4th ed.). Routledge.

Stroebe, M., & Schut, H. (1999). The dual process model of coping with bereavement: Rationale and description. Death Studies, 23(3), 197–224.

Worden, J. W. (2018). Grief counseling and grief therapy: A handbook for the mental health practitioner (5th ed.). Springer Publishing Company.

Chapter 4

Grieving as a Family

Navigating Shared Loss - While Honoring Individual Grief

Loss rarely belongs to only one person. When someone dies, an entire network of relationships is affected. Families often grieve together, yet each person carries the loss in their own way.

The Dynamics of Family Grief

How Each Member Grieves Differently

No two people grieve in exactly the same way, and this is especially true within families. Each family member's grief is shaped by their relationship to the deceased, their personality, and their coping mechanisms. These differences can lead to misunderstandings and conflicts, as family members may struggle to understand or support one another's grief (Worden, 2018).

The Role of Relationships

The relationship each family member had with the person who died strongly influences how grief is experienced. A spouse may mourn the loss of companionship and shared daily routines, while a child may grieve the loss of guidance or protection. Siblings may mourn shared history, while parents often experience grief intertwined with identity and responsibility.

Because these relationships differ, family members may experience distinct emotional responses. At times, this can create tension, particularly if one person feels their grief is not being recognized or understood by others.

The Role of Personality

Personality also influences how grief is expressed. Some people respond to loss openly, speaking about memories and emotions as they arise. Others turn inward, processing grief privately or maintaining routines that provide stability during a difficult time.

These patterns are sometimes described as different grieving styles, some people experience grief primarily through emotional expression, while others cope through action, reflection, or problem-solving (Doka & Martin, 2010). Neither approach is more valid than the other. They simply represent different ways of carrying the emotional weight of loss.

Differences in grieving style can create misunderstandings within families. Someone who speaks openly about grief may interpret silence as emotional distance, while a quieter mourner may feel overwhelmed by constant discussion of the loss.

Different Paths Through Grief

After their father died, Maria and her brother Daniel found themselves grieving in very different ways. Maria wanted to talk about him constantly. She shared stories at family dinners, looked through old photographs, and often mentioned the small habits that reminded her of him. Talking about their father made her feel connected to him.

Daniel responded differently. He rarely brought up their father's name and returned quickly to his daily routines. He spent longer hours at work and avoided conversations that focused on the loss. To Maria, his silence felt like indifference. She wondered how he could seem so unaffected.

What she did not realize was that Daniel's quiet distance was his way of coping. Speaking about the loss made the reality feel overwhelming. Staying busy helped him manage emotions he struggled to express.

Over time, both siblings began to understand that their reactions reflected different personalities rather than different levels of love. Maria's openness and Daniel's quiet resilience were simply two ways of carrying the same grief.

The Role of Coping Mechanisms

People also cope with loss in different ways. Some turn toward spiritual practices or religious traditions. Others seek counseling, creative expression, or conversations with trusted friends. Still others focus on responsibilities and routines as they gradually adjust to the absence of the person who died.

Grief often involves shifting between confronting the emotional pain of loss and managing the practical demands of daily life (Stroebe & Schut, 1999). Within families, these different coping patterns can sometimes be misinterpreted as avoidance or emotional distance.

Recognizing that people cope in different ways can help families approach one another with greater patience and understanding during a time when compassion is needed most.

Supporting Each Other Through Loss

Finding Unity in Shared Pain

Despite the challenges of family grief, shared loss can also be a source of connection and unity. By supporting one another through the grieving process, family members can find strength in their shared pain and create a sense of solidarity that helps them navigate the difficult journey of grief (Worden, 2018).

Open Communication

Open communication is essential for supporting one another through grief. Family members should be encouraged to express their emotions and needs, even if they differ from those of others. This open communication can help prevent misunderstandings and conflicts, as each family member will have a better understanding of what the others are going through.

Shared Rituals

Shared rituals, such as memorial services or family gatherings, can also provide a sense of unity and connection. These rituals can help family members honor the memory of the deceased and find comfort in one another's presence (Neimeyer, 2012). These rituals work best when they allow space for each family member's needs and preferences.

Seeking Professional Help

At times, grief may strain family relationships or reopen long-standing tensions. When communication becomes difficult or conflict grows, outside support can be helpful. Family counseling offers a structured space where individuals can speak openly, explore differences in grieving styles, and learn healthier ways to support one another. With guidance, families often discover that understanding one another's grief can become a path toward renewed connection (Doka & Martin, 2010).

When Grief Divides

Navigating Conflicts That Arise from Loss

While shared loss can bring families together, it can also drive them apart. Conflicts can arise when family members grieve differently, have unresolved issues, or struggle to meet one another's needs. These conflicts can be particularly painful, as they compound the pain of loss with the pain of division.

Unresolved Issues

When relationships with the person who died were complicated, grief may carry additional layers of emotion. A family member who experienced conflict with the deceased may struggle with guilt, anger, or regret. These feelings can surface unexpectedly and may influence interactions with other family members.

Families sometimes find that old disagreements resurface during the grieving process. Conversations about the past, decisions about memorials, or differing interpretations of family history can reopen unresolved wounds. Addressing these emotions honestly—sometimes with the support of counseling—can help families move toward greater understanding and healing (Neimeyer, 2012).

Differing Needs

Grief rarely unfolds in the same way for everyone. One family member may want to speak openly about the person who died, while another may find those conversations overwhelming. Some individuals seek closeness during grief, while others need solitude.

These differences do not mean family members care less about the loss. They reflect the many ways people adapt to grief and manage emotional pain (Stroebe & Schut, 1999). When families recognize that grieving styles differ, they are often better able to respect one another's needs without interpreting those differences as rejection or indifference.

The Role of Boundaries

Healthy boundaries can help families maintain connection while honoring individual coping needs. A grieving person may need time alone, limits on certain conversations, or space from family expectations. Respecting those boundaries can prevent additional strain during an already difficult period.

Boundaries do not create distance within a family; they often make continued relationships possible. When family members acknowledge one another's limits with compassion, they create an environment where each person can grieve in their own way while remaining part of the larger family network.

Conclusion

Grief unfolds differently for every person, shaped by relationships, personality, and circumstance. Within families, these differences may create both moments of tension and opportunities for deeper understanding.

Recognizing that grief has many expressions allows families to approach one another with greater patience and empathy. Although loss can reveal divisions, it can also strengthen bonds as family members learn to support one another through one of life's most difficult experiences.

Exercise: The Family Grief Map

Purpose:

To help families understand how each member experiences and expresses grief differently, identify overlapping needs, and find ways to support one another without judgment.

Materials Needed:

A large sheet of paper or whiteboard

Colored pens or markers

Optional: Sticky notes for flexibility

Step 1: Create the Map

Draw a large circle in the middle of the page labeled "Our Family." Around it, draw smaller circles for each family member. Write their names inside.

Step 2: Individual Reflections

Ask each family member to take five minutes to think about:

How they've been feeling since the loss (sad, angry, numb, disconnected, etc.)

How they tend to show or hide those feelings

What they need most right now from others (space, conversation, reassurance, time alone, shared memories, etc.)

Step 3: Add to the Map

Using different colors, write or draw inside each person's circle:

Emotions: (blue for sadness, red for anger, green for hope, etc.)

Coping habits: journaling, talking, keeping busy, silence, etc.

Support needs: what helps or doesn't help when others try to comfort them

Step 4: Find the Crossroads

As a group, look for connections.

Are two people grieving in similar ways but not realizing it?

Is someone's silence being misread as disinterest?

Is anyone's coping style unintentionally causing distance?

Highlight areas where mutual understanding could help. These are your "crossroads" — opportunities to heal together rather than apart.

Step 5: Family Check-In

Agree on a few shared practices to support one another, such as:

A short weekly family check-in about emotions

A shared memory activity (like creating a scrapbook or cooking a favorite meal of the loved one)

Respecting individual needs without taking them personally

Reflection Prompt:

Write or discuss it together:

"What have I learned about the way each of us grieves? How can I honor both our differences and our shared love for the person we lost?"

References

Doka, K. J., & Martin, T. L. (2010). *Grieving beyond gender: Understanding the ways men and women mourn.* Routledge.

Neimeyer, R. A. (2012). *Techniques of grief therapy: Creative practices for counseling the bereaved.* Routledge.

Neimeyer, R. A. (2016). Techniques of Grief Therapy: Assessment and Intervention. Routledge.

Stroebe, M., Schut, H., & Stroebe, W. (2007). Health Outcomes of Bereavement. The Lancet, 370(9603), 1960-1973.

Worden, J. W. (2018). Grief Counseling and Grief Therapy: A Handbook for the Mental Health Practitioner. Springer Publishing Company.

Worden, J. W. (2018). *Grief counseling and grief therapy: A handbook for the mental health practitioner* (5th ed.). Springer Publishing Company.

Chapter 5

The Physical Side of Grief

How Loss Impacts Your Body and Health

Grief is often thought of as an emotional experience, but its impact extends far beyond the mind. The physical toll of grief can be profound, affecting every system in the body and manifesting in a wide range of symptoms. From fatigue and changes in appetite to sleep disturbances and weakened immunity, the body bears the weight of loss in ways that are both visible and invisible.

The Mind-Body Connection

How Grief Manifests Physically

The mind and body are deeply interconnected, and grief is a powerful example of this connection. When we experience loss, the emotional pain we feel is not confined to the mind; it reverberates throughout the body, triggering a cascade of physiological responses. These responses are part of the body's natural reaction to stress, but when grief is prolonged or intense, they can take a significant toll on physical health.

The Stress Response and Grief

Grief activates the body's stress response, also known as the fight-or-flight response. This reaction is regulated by the sympathetic nervous system, which releases stress hormones such as cortisol and adrenaline into the bloodstream (O'Connor, 2019). These hormones prepare the body to respond to a perceived threat, increasing heart rate, blood pressure, and muscle tension.

In short bursts, this response is protective. It allows the body to respond quickly to danger. During periods of prolonged emotional stress, however, sustained activation of this system can strain multiple bodily systems. Extended stress exposure has been associated with cardiovascular changes, digestive disturbances, sleep disruption, and reduced immune efficiency (Stroebe, Schut, & Stroebe, 2007).

Many grieving individuals therefore notice persistent fatigue, disrupted sleep patterns, or a general sense that their bodies feel depleted.

The Role of the Brain

Brain activity also shifts during grief. The amygdala, which plays an important role in processing emotional experiences, becomes highly responsive following a significant loss. At the same time, the prefrontal cortex, responsible for planning, decision-making, and emotional regulation, may function less efficiently during periods of intense emotional distress (Shear, 2015).

This temporary imbalance can make concentration difficult. People often describe feeling mentally scattered, forgetful, or unable to focus on routine tasks. Physical symptoms such as headaches, dizziness, and mental fatigue may accompany this cognitive strain.

Emotional symptoms, including irritability, anxiety, or persistent sadness, may also intensify during this period, further reinforcing the interaction between psychological stress and physical well-being.

The Immune System and Grief

Bereavement can also affect immune functioning. Studies have shown that people who are grieving may experience greater vulnerability to illness during the months following a loss (Stroebe, Schut, & Stroebe, 2007). Stress hormones, disrupted sleep, and changes in daily habits, such as irregular meals or reduced physical activity, can all influence immune response.

For many individuals, these physical changes gradually stabilize as the body adjusts to the emotional strain of loss. Recognizing these symptoms as part of the grieving process can help people respond with patience and self-care rather than concern that something is "wrong."

Fatigue, Appetite Changes, and Sleep Disturbances

Common Physical Symptoms of Grief

The physical effects of grief can be as noticeable as the emotional ones. Many people experience persistent fatigue, changes in appetite, or disrupted sleep during the weeks and months following a loss. These symptoms can interfere with daily routines, making ordinary tasks feel far more difficult than usual. Physical exhaustion often accompanies the emotional strain of adapting to life after loss.

Fatigue: The Weight of Grief

Fatigue is one of the most frequently reported physical symptoms during bereavement. Many grieving individuals describe a deep exhaustion that sleep alone does not fully relieve. Emotional strain, stress hormones, and disrupted routines can leave both the mind and body depleted (Stroebe, Schut, & Stroebe, 2007).

Several factors contribute to this exhaustion. Elevated stress hormones place sustained demands on the body's energy systems, while changes in sleep patterns prevent full physical recovery. Emotional strain also requires considerable mental effort as individuals process memories, adjust to new responsibilities, and navigate unfamiliar daily routines.

Fatigue often becomes more noticeable when everyday responsibilities continue despite the loss. Work obligations, family care, and household tasks may feel overwhelming during a period when emotional energy is already limited. As a result, many grieving individuals find themselves caught between the need to rest and the practical demands of daily life.

This exhaustion does not indicate weakness or lack of resilience. It reflects the body's response to prolonged emotional stress and the effort required to adjust to profound change.

Appetite Changes

The Body's Response to Loss

Grief often alters eating patterns. Some individuals lose interest in food entirely, struggling to eat even small meals. Others notice the opposite response and find themselves eating more frequently, sometimes turning to food for comfort.

These shifts are closely connected to the body's stress response. Cortisol, one of the primary stress hormones, can suppress appetite during periods of acute stress but increase hunger when stress persists (O'Connor, 2019). As a result, many grieving individuals experience fluctuating eating patterns, alternating between little interest in food and cravings for high-calorie or sugary foods.

Emotional factors also influence appetite during grief. For some people, eating may feel strangely incompatible with mourning, as if moments of enjoyment conflict with the seriousness of their loss. Others may experience brief comfort while eating, using familiar foods to create a sense of normalcy during an otherwise painful period.

Sleep Disturbances: The Nighttime Struggle

Sleep difficulties are another common physical response to grief. Many people experience insomnia, lying awake long after bedtime or waking repeatedly during the night. Others notice the opposite pattern, sleeping for extended periods yet still waking with persistent fatigue.

Several factors contribute to these disturbances. Emotional distress can make it difficult for the mind to settle at night, while elevated stress hormones interfere with the body's natural sleep–wake cycle. Intrusive memories or vivid dreams about the loss may also interrupt sleep, leaving the grieving person restless and unrefreshed.

When sleep becomes irregular, the effects often extend beyond nighttime. Poor sleep can intensify fatigue, weaken immune response, and reduce concentration during the day (Stroebe, Schut, & Stroebe, 2007). Emotional resilience may also decline, making grief feel heavier and more difficult to manage.

Caring for Your Body While Grieving

Practical Self-Care Tips

The physical effects of grief can feel overwhelming, particularly when exhaustion, disrupted sleep, or appetite changes begin to interfere with daily life. While self-care cannot remove the pain of loss, caring for the body can help stabilize energy, support emotional resilience, and ease some of the strain that grief places on the mind and body (Stroebe, Schut, & Stroebe, 2007).

Prioritize Rest and Sleep

Rest is essential for healing, both physically and emotionally. Grieving individuals should prioritize sleep, even if it feels difficult or elusive. Creating a calming bedtime routine, such as reading a book or taking a warm bath, can help signal to the body that it is time to rest. Avoiding caffeine, alcohol, and screens before bed can also improve sleep quality.

For those struggling with insomnia, relaxation techniques such as deep breathing, meditation, or progressive muscle relaxation can help calm the mind and prepare the body for sleep. If sleep disturbances persist, it may be helpful to consult a healthcare provider or sleep specialist.

Nourish Your Body

Proper nutrition is crucial for maintaining physical health during grief. Even when appetite is low, it is important to eat regular, balanced meals to provide the body with the energy and nutrients it needs. Small, frequent meals may be easier to manage than large ones, and focusing on nutrient-dense foods such as fruits, vegetables, lean proteins, and whole grains can help support overall health.

For those who find it difficult to eat, drinking smoothies or soups can provide essential nutrients without requiring a large appetite. Staying hydrated is also important, as dehydration can exacerbate fatigue and other physical symptoms.

Move Your Body

Gentle movement can support both physical and emotional well-being during grief. Physical activity stimulates the release of endorphins, natural chemicals that support mood regulation and stress reduction.

Exercise does not need to be strenuous to be beneficial. Walking, stretching, yoga, or light outdoor activity can help restore energy and improve sleep patterns. Movement also offers a structured way to release tension that often accumulates in the body during periods of emotional stress.

Regular activity has been associated with improved mood and stress regulation, which can support overall adjustment during bereavement (Stroebe & Schut, 1999).

Seek Professional Support

For some individuals, the physical symptoms of grief become severe or persistent. Ongoing sleep disruption, prolonged appetite loss, chronic fatigue, or physical illness may require professional attention.

Healthcare providers can evaluate physical symptoms and recommend strategies to support recovery. Counseling or grief therapy can also help individuals address the connection between emotional stress and physical health. Therapeutic support often provides space to process the loss, develop coping strategies, and gradually restore emotional balance (Worden, 2018).

Practice Self-Compassion

Perhaps the most important aspect of self-care during grief is self-compassion. The physical and emotional symptoms of grief can feel discouraging, especially when energy is low and progress seems slow. These reactions are not signs of weakness; they are part of the body's response to profound loss.

Allowing space for rest, accepting help from others, and recognizing personal limits can reduce unnecessary pressure during a vulnerable time. Healing rarely follows a predictable timeline. Offering oneself patience and understanding can make the path through grief more manageable.

Conclusion

The physical side of grief is often overlooked, but it is an essential part of the grieving process. The mind-body connection means that emotional pain can manifest physically, affecting every system in the body and leading to symptoms such as fatigue, appetite changes, and sleep disturbances. By understanding these physical symptoms and taking steps to care for the body, grieving individuals can support their overall health and create a foundation for healing.

While grief is a deeply personal and often painful experience, it is also a testament to the power of love and connection. By honoring the body's needs and practicing self-care, grieving individuals can begin to navigate the weight of loss and find a path toward healing and hope.

Exercise: The Seasons of Healing Journal

Purpose:

To help you recognize that grief moves in cycles rather than straight lines, and to reflect on how your emotions and healing evolve over time.

Materials Needed:

A notebook or journal

Colored pens or pencils (optional)

A quiet space for reflection

Step 1: Create Your Seasons Page

Draw four large boxes or circles labeled Winter, Spring, Summer, and Fall.

These represent emotional seasons, not literal ones.

Winter – Stillness, numbness, survival

Spring – Small signs of hope or renewal

Summer – Growth, laughter, reconnection

Fall – Reflection, sadness mixed with gratitude

Step 2: Reflect on Each Season

Think back on your grief journey so far. Where have you been? Where are you now?

In each box, write:

Words that describe how you felt during that phase

Events, people, or triggers that marked that period

What helped you move through it

Example:

Winter: I couldn't get out of bed some days. Avoided friends. Felt like time stopped.

Spring: Started walking again. Reconnected with family. Felt sunlight differently.

Step 3: Identify Patterns

Look at your "seasons." Notice:

Do certain times of year or dates bring harder emotions?

Are there repeating cycles of sadness followed by brief peace?

What helps you shift from one season to another?

Step 4: Set Gentle Intentions

Write one sentence for each season starting with "When I'm in this season again, I will…"

Example:

"When I'm in Winter again, I'll remember that stillness doesn't mean failure."

"When I reach Spring, I'll allow joy without guilt."

Step 5: Revisit Over Time

Return to this exercise every few months. Add new reflections or new "seasons" as your healing changes. Seeing your growth on paper can help you release the pressure to be "over it."

Reflection Prompt:

"If grief were a cycle of seasons, which one am I in today—and what can I give myself permission to feel here?"

References

Neimeyer, R. A. (2016). Techniques of Grief Therapy: Assessment and Intervention. Routledge.

O'Connor, M. F. (2019). Grief: A Brief History of Research on How Body, Mind, and Brain Adapt. Psychosomatic Medicine, 81(8), 731-738.

Schut, M. S. H. (1999). The dual process model of coping with bereavement: Rationale and description. *Death studies*, *23*(3), 197-224.

Shear, M. K. (2015). Complicated Grief. New England Journal of Medicine, 372(2), 153-160.

Stroebe, M., Schut, H., & Stroebe, W. (2007). Health Outcomes of Bereavement. The Lancet, 370(9603), 1960-1973.

Worden, J. W. (2018). Grief Counseling and Grief Therapy: A Handbook for the Mental Health Practitioner. Springer Publishing Company.

Part 2: Navigating the Pain

Chapter 6

When Grief Feels Stuck

Recognizing and Addressing Complicated Grief

Grief is a natural response to loss, a process that, while painful, allows individuals to come to terms with their new reality. However, for some, grief does not follow a linear path. Instead, it becomes entrenched, overwhelming, and seemingly unending. This is known as complicated grief, a condition that can disrupt daily functioning and hinder the healing process.

.

What Is Complicated Grief?

Understanding When Grief Becomes Overwhelming

Complicated grief is different from the natural ebb and flow of typical mourning. While acute grief is characterized by intense sadness, longing, and disbelief that gradually lessen over months, complicated grief persists and often intensifies over time. It may show up as chronic longing, difficulty accepting the death, preoccupation with the deceased, or a feeling that life has permanently lost meaning (Shear, 2015).

The Diagnostic and Statistical Manual of Mental Disorders (5th ed.; DSM-5) describes this condition as Persistent Complex Bereavement Disorder, involving persistent, pervasive grief reactions that exceed social, cultural, or religious norms for a person's background (American Psychiatric Association [APA], 2013). Individuals with complicated grief may appear "stuck," unable to adapt to life without their loved one.

Studies indicate that what is now termed Prolonged Grief Disorder, affects approximately 7-10% of bereaved individuals (Prigerson et al., 2021). It is more likely to develop after sudden, violent, or traumatic losses—such as accidents, suicides, or unexpected deaths, but can also occur following anticipated deaths when unresolved guilt, dependency, or conflict exist (Prigerson & Maciejewski, 2008).

Emotional and Behavioral Symptoms

Recognizing complicated grief involves noting certain persistent patterns. Common signs include:

- Intense, prolonged yearning for the person who died.
- Frequent preoccupation with the death or the deceased.

- Difficulty accepting the reality of the loss.
- Feelings of emptiness or a sense that life is devoid of meaning.
- Either avoiding reminders of the loss or being unable to part with possessions.
- Social withdrawal and emotional numbness.
- Persistent guilt or self-blame.
- Intrusive thoughts or recurring dreams about the deceased.

These symptoms can last for months or years, causing significant distress and interfering with work, relationships, or health (Zisook & Shear, 2009). Although complicated grief and depression can overlap, depression often involves a broader loss of interest, whereas complicated grief centers on the loss itself (Shear, 2015).

Why Grief Gets Stuck

Understanding the Underlying Mechanisms

Complicated grief often arises from a mix of psychological, neurological, and social factors that influence how we process loss.

Attachment and the Brain

Human attachment is deeply rooted in our brains. When a loved one dies, the attachment system, which once provided security, is disrupted. Research shows that individuals with complicated grief display heightened activity in the brain's nucleus accumbens—a region associated with craving and reward (O'Connor et al., 2008). In essence, the brain continues to "seek" the lost person, similar to how cravings work in addiction.

Meanwhile, the amygdala—responsible for processing fear—remains highly active, while the prefrontal cortex, which helps regulate emotions, struggles to balance these responses (O'Connor, 2019). This imbalance can leave a person trapped in a cycle of longing and distress.

Cognitive and Emotional Traps

Emotionally, complicated grief often arises when the mind cannot reconcile two opposing realities: the permanence of death and the persistence of love. Many individuals cling to mental representations of the deceased, unable to integrate the loss into their life narrative (Neimeyer, 2012).

Cognitive distortions such as guilt ("I should have done more"), catastrophizing ("I'll never be happy again"), or idealization ("They were perfect") can perpetuate grief. These thought patterns prevent emotional processing, keeping the mourner suspended between denial and despair (Boelen, 2016).

Social and Cultural Factors

Broader social expectations can also complicate grief. In cultures that emphasize quick recovery, mourners may suppress emotions to appear "strong," unintentionally prolonging grief. Doka (2002) described this as disenfranchised grief, a form of mourning that society does not acknowledge. When people feel their grief is invalidated or unseen, it can become more entrenched.

Recognizing When to Seek Help

Understanding the Difference Between Grieving and Suffering in Isolation

Because grief is personal, it can be challenging to identify when it has become complicated. However, certain signs suggest it's time to seek professional support:

- Persistent, intense grief that lasts more than 6–12 months without improvement.
- Difficulty functioning—struggles with work, relationships, or daily tasks.
- Avoiding reminders of the deceased—or, conversely, an inability to part with reminders.
- Feelings of emptiness, hopelessness, or a belief that life lacks meaning.
- Thoughts of self-harm or a desire to join the deceased.
- Physical symptoms like chronic fatigue, insomnia, or frequent illness.

If these symptoms persist, reaching out to a mental health professional, especially one trained in grief therapy. is crucial. Complicated grief isn't a personal failure; it's a treatable condition.

Therapeutic Approaches for Complicated Grief

Complicated Grief Therapy (CGT)

Developed by Dr. Katherine Shear and colleagues, Complicated Grief Therapy (CGT) is one of the most evidence-based treatments for this condition. CGT integrates cognitive-behavioral techniques, exposure therapy, and elements of attachment theory to help individuals accept the reality of the loss and reengage with life (Shear, 2015).

CGT typically involves exploring the relationship with the deceased, revisiting painful memories in a safe setting, and restoring life goals. Clinical trials show that CGT significantly reduces symptoms compared to traditional psychotherapy or medication alone (Shear et al., 2005).

Cognitive-Behavioral Therapy (CBT)

CBT helps individuals identify and challenge maladaptive thoughts that maintain grief, such as guilt or self-blame. Techniques like journaling, thought restructuring, and exposure to avoided situations promote emotional processing (Boelen, 2016).

Group and Peer Support

Group therapy and peer-based bereavement support can be profoundly healing. Hearing others' experiences helps normalize emotions and reduce isolation. Studies show that sharing grief in supportive groups fosters emotional regulation and posttraumatic growth (Neimeyer, 2012).

Mindfulness and Acceptance-Based Interventions

Mindfulness practices teach individuals to observe grief without judgment. By focusing on the present moment, mindfulness can reduce rumination and increase self-compassion (Kabat-Zinn, 2003). Acceptance and Commitment Therapy (ACT), a related approach, emphasizes finding meaning while coexisting with pain (Hayes et al., 2006).

Pharmacological Support

In some cases, medication may be prescribed to address comorbid depression or anxiety. Antidepressants can help regulate mood and energy levels, allowing individuals to engage more effectively in therapy (Zisook & Shear, 2009). Medication, however, should be seen as one component of a broader treatment plan.

Breaking the Cycle: Steps Toward Healing

While professional support is invaluable, there are also self-guided steps that can complement therapy and promote recovery. Healing from complicated grief involves re-establishing balance—emotionally, socially, and physically.

1. Acknowledge the Reality of the Loss

Denial serves as a temporary buffer, but long-term avoidance prolongs suffering. Naming the loss—speaking it aloud, journaling about it, or discussing it in therapy—helps integrate it into one's life story (Worden, 2018).

2. Reconnect with Support Networks

Isolation feeds despair. Whether through family, friends, or bereavement groups, connection reminds the grieving person that they are not alone. Social support is one of the strongest predictors of resilience after loss (Stroebe et al., 2007).

3. Rebuild Routine and Purpose

Daily structure restores a sense of stability. Simple habits—morning walks, regular meals, small tasks—can anchor the body and mind when everything else feels uncertain. Setting small, achievable goals builds momentum and reintroduces agency.

4. Express Emotion Safely

Suppressing emotion can lead to prolonged distress. Creative outlets such as writing, painting, or music can help externalize grief, making it more manageable (Neimeyer, 2012).

5. Practice Mindfulness and Self-Compassion

Grief often brings self-criticism ("I should be over this by now"). Mindfulness teaches presence; self-compassion offers grace. Together, they foster acceptance of both pain and progress (Kabat-Zinn, 2003).

6. Honor the Deceased

Rituals—planting a tree, lighting a candle, volunteering in the person's memory transform grief into meaning. Maintaining continuing bonds does not impede healing; it can sustain it (Klass, Silverman, & Nickman, 1996).

7. Reframe Healing as Integration, Not Erasure

Healing does not mean forgetting or "moving on." It means integrating the loss into one's evolving identity. Grief work involves reconstructing meaning, understanding who we are in the world after loss (Neimeyer, 2012).

The Path Forward

Complicated grief can make the future feel impossible, but healing is attainable. With the right support, therapeutic guidance, community connection, and self-compassion individuals can transform persistent sorrow into remembrance, love, and renewed life. The journey is not about returning to who you were before the loss but about discovering who you can become after it.

As one grief counselor said, "The pain doesn't leave you, but it learns to walk beside you." That companionship between loss and love is where healing begins.

Exercise: Naming the Faces of My Grief

Purpose:

To help you recognize, name, and accept the many emotions that come with grief—anger, fear, sadness, guilt, numbness, and even relief—without judging any of them as "right" or "wrong."

Materials Needed:

Paper or journal

Pen or colored pencils

Optional: a mirror or photo of yourself

Step 1: Create Your Emotional Portrait

Draw a large outline of a face on your page. It doesn't need to be perfect—just a simple sketch that represents you.

Around or inside the face, write the different emotions you've felt since your loss. Examples:

- Anger
- Confusion
- Numbness
- Fear
- Hope
- Guilt
- Peace

Use colors if you can: red for anger, blue for sadness, gray for numbness, yellow for hope, etc.

Step 2: Give Each Emotion a Voice

For every emotion you wrote, finish this sentence in your journal:

"My [emotion] says…"

Example:

"My anger says, 'This isn't fair.'"

"My guilt says, 'I should have done more.'"

"My sadness says, 'I miss what we had.'"

This step lets you listen to what each feeling is trying to tell you rather than suppressing it.

Step 3: Reflect on Relationships Between Emotions

Notice which emotions appear together or seem to clash. Ask yourself:

Do I tend to favor one emotion (like anger) to avoid another (like sadness)?

Which emotions do I hide from others?

Which ones do I express openly?

Circle or highlight the emotions that feel the hardest to face.

Step 4: Acceptance Statement

Under your drawing, write this affirmation:

"All my emotions have a place in my healing. None of them define me—they only help me understand my loss."

You can also rewrite it in your own words if you prefer.

Step 5: Optional Mirror Work

Look at yourself in the mirror and say aloud the emotion that feels strongest right now. Example:

"I see your sadness, and it's okay."

"I see your anger, and it's safe to feel it."

Even thirty seconds of acknowledgment can ease emotional resistance and bring calm.

Reflection Prompt:

"Which emotion do I resist the most, and what might it be trying to protect me from?"

References

American Psychiatric Association. (2013). Diagnostic and statistical manual of mental disorders (5th ed.). Author.

Boelen, P. A. (2016). Improving the understanding and treatment of complex grief: An important issue for psychotraumatology. European Journal of Psychotraumatology, 7(1), 32609.

Doka, K. J. (2002). Disenfranchised grief: Recognizing hidden sorrow. Lexington Books.

Hayes, S. C., Strosahl, K. D., & Wilson, K. G. (2006). Acceptance and commitment therapy: An experiential approach to behavior change. Guilford Press.

Kabat-Zinn, J. (2003). Mindfulness-based interventions in context: Past, present, and future. Clinical Psychology: Science and Practice, 10(2), 144–156.

Klass, D., Silverman, P. R., & Nickman, S. L. (Eds.). (1996). Continuing bonds: New understandings of grief. Taylor & Francis.

Neimeyer, R. A. (2012). Techniques of grief therapy: Creative practices for counseling the bereaved. Routledge.

O'Connor, M.-F. (2019). Grief: A brief history of research on how body, mind, and brain adapt. Psychosomatic Medicine, 81(8), 731–738.

O'Connor, M.-F., Wellisch, D. K., Stanton, A. L., Eisenberger, N. I., Irwin, M. R., & Lieberman, M. D. (2008). Craving love? Enduring grief activates brain's reward center. NeuroImage, 42(2), 969–972.

Prigerson, H. G., & Maciejewski, P. K. (2008). Grief and acceptance as opposite sides of the same coin: Setting a research agenda to study peaceful acceptance of loss. British Journal of Psychiatry, 193(6), 435–437.

Prigerson, H. G., Kakarala, S., Gang, J., & Maciejewski, P. K. (2021). History and status of prolonged grief disorder as a psychiatric diagnosis. *Annual review of clinical psychology*, *17*(1), 109-126.

Shear, M. K. (2015). Complicated grief treatment: The theory, practice, and outcomes. Depression and Anxiety, 32(8), 553–560.

Shear, M. K., Frank, E., Houck, P. R., & Reynolds, C. F. (2005). Treatment of complicated grief: A randomized controlled trial. JAMA, 293(21), 2601–2608.

Shear, M. K., Simon, N., Wall, M., Zisook, S., Neimeyer, R., Duan, N., … Keshaviah, A. (2011). Complicated grief and related bereavement issues for DSM-5. Depression and Anxiety, 28(2), 103–117.

Stroebe, M., Schut, H., & Stroebe, W. (2007). Health outcomes of bereavement. The Lancet, 370(9603), 1960–1973.

Worden, J. W. (2018). Grief counseling and grief therapy: A handbook for the mental health practitioner (5th ed.). Springer Publishing Company.

Zisook, S., & Shear, K. (2009). Grief and bereavement: What psychiatrists need to know. World Psychiatry, 8(2), 67–74.

Chapter 7

The Role of Therapy and Support Groups

Finding Professional and Communal Help

Therapy and support groups play a vital role in the grieving process, offering individuals the opportunity to explore their emotions, gain insight, and connect with others who understand their pain.

The Benefits of Therapy

How Talking Helps Heal

Therapy provides a safe and supportive environment for individuals to express their emotions, process their grief, and develop coping strategies. The benefits of therapy for grief are well-documented, with research showing that it can reduce symptoms of depression, anxiety, and complicated grief (Neimeyer & Currier, 2009).

One of the key benefits of therapy is the opportunity to talk openly about your feelings. Grief can be isolating, and many people feel that others do not understand their pain. A therapist can provide a non-judgmental space where you can share your thoughts and emotions without fear of criticism or rejection.

Therapy can also help you gain insight into your grief. A trained therapist can help you identify patterns of thought or behavior that may be contributing to your pain and work with you to develop healthier coping mechanisms. For example, cognitive-behavioral therapy (CBT) can help you challenge negative thoughts and beliefs about your loss, while acceptance and commitment therapy (ACT) can help you accept your emotions and commit to actions that align with your values.

In addition to individual therapy, group therapy can be a valuable resource for those experiencing grief. Group therapy provides a sense of community and understanding, as participants share their experiences and support one another. This can be particularly helpful for those who feel isolated in their grief.

Finding the Right Support Group

Connecting with Others Who Understand

Support groups offer a unique opportunity to connect with others who are experiencing similar losses. These groups can provide a sense of community, understanding, and validation, which can be incredibly healing.

When looking for a support group, it is important to find one that aligns with your needs and preferences. Here are some factors to consider:

Type of Loss: Some support groups are specific to certain types of loss, such as the death of a spouse, child, or parent. Others may be more general, catering to a wide range of losses. Consider what type of loss you are grieving and look for a group that focuses on that experience.

Format: Support groups can vary in format, from in-person meetings to online forums. Consider what format would be most comfortable and accessible for you.

Facilitator: Some support groups are led by trained professionals, such as therapists or counselors, while others are peer-led. Consider whether you would prefer a professionally facilitated group or one that is led by peers.

Size: The size of the group can impact the level of intimacy and support you receive. Some people prefer smaller groups where they can share more openly, while others may feel more comfortable in larger groups.

Frequency: Consider how often the group meets and whether that fits with your schedule and needs.

Location: If you are considering an in-person group, think about the location and whether it is convenient for you to attend.

Cost: Some support groups are free, while others may charge a fee. Consider your budget and whether the cost is manageable for you.

Once you have found a support group that meets your needs, give it a try. It may take a few sessions to feel comfortable, but many people find that the support and understanding they receive from the group are invaluable in their healing process.

Alternative Therapies

Art, Music, and Other Creative Outlets for Grief

In addition to traditional therapy and support groups, alternative therapies can offer unique ways to process and express grief. Creative outlets such as art, music, and writing can provide a means of expressing emotions that may be difficult to put into words.

Art Therapy: Art therapy involves the use of creative techniques such as drawing, painting, or sculpting to express emotions and explore grief. This form of therapy can be particularly helpful for those who find it difficult to articulate their feelings verbally. Art therapy can provide a safe and non-judgmental space to explore complex emotions and gain insight into the grieving process (Malchiodi, 2012).

Music Therapy: Music therapy uses music to address emotional, cognitive, and social needs. This can include listening to music, playing instruments, or composing songs. Music has a powerful ability to evoke emotions and memories, making it a valuable tool for processing grief. Music therapy can help individuals express their emotions, find comfort, and connect with others (Hilliard, 2001).

Writing Therapy: Writing therapy, also known as expressive writing, involves writing about your thoughts and feelings related to grief. This can take the form of journaling, poetry, or letter writing. Writing can help process emotions, gain clarity, and reflect on your experiences. Expressive writing can reduce grief symptoms and improve emotional well-being (Pennebaker & Seagal, 1999).

Dance/Movement Therapy: Dance/movement therapy uses movement to express emotions and explore grief. This form of therapy can help individuals connect with their bodies, release pent-up emotions, and find release and relief. Dance/movement therapy can be particularly helpful for those who find it difficult to express their emotions verbally (Levy, 1988).

Nature Therapy: Nature therapy, also known as ecotherapy, involves spending time in nature to promote healing and well-being. This can include activities such as hiking, gardening, or simply spending time outdoors. Nature therapy can provide peace and connection, helping individuals find solace and perspective in the natural world (Berger & McLeod, 2006).

These alternative therapies can be used in conjunction with traditional therapy or as standalone approaches to grief. They offer unique ways to process and express emotions, providing a holistic approach to healing.

Conclusion

Navigating the pain of grief is a deeply personal and often challenging journey. For those experiencing complicated grief, the path may feel endless and overwhelming. However, by recognizing the signs of complicated grief, seeking professional help, and exploring various therapeutic approaches, individuals can begin to break the cycle of endless sorrow and move toward healing.

Therapy and support groups offer valuable resources for those struggling with grief, providing a safe space to explore emotions, gain insight, and connect with others. Alternative therapies, such as art, music, and writing, offer creative outlets for expressing and processing grief, providing a holistic approach to healing.

Ultimately, the journey through grief is unique to each individual. There is no right or wrong way to grieve, and healing takes time. By taking steps to seek help, connect with others, and explore creative outlets, individuals can navigate the pain of grief and find a path toward acceptance and healing.

Exercise: Building a Family Memory Ritual

Purpose:

To help families stay connected through shared remembrance, mutual support, and open communication—without forcing anyone to grieve the same way.

Materials Needed:

A candle, photo, or meaningful object that represents your loved one

Paper and pens

Optional: a jar, box, or small basket

Step 1: Create a Safe Space

Gather as a family in a comfortable, quiet place. Agree that this is a space without judgment. Each person can share or remain silent participation is by choice, not obligation.

Step 2: Shared Reflection

Ask each person to write down or say aloud:

One thing they miss most about the person

One thing they are grateful for having experienced together

One way they try to keep that memory alive

You can go around the group or let people speak naturally as they feel ready.

Step 3: The Memory Jar (or Box)

After everyone shares, place your written memories into a jar or box. This becomes your Family Memory Jar.

You can add to it anytime—birthdays, holidays, anniversaries, or random days when the memory surfaces.

Over time, it grows into a living archive of connection and healing.

Optional variation: write the memories on different colored paper each color can represent a different emotion (love, gratitude, sadness, laughter).

Step 4: Create a Gentle Ritual

Choose a recurring moment—a Sunday dinner, birthday, or seasonal change when you'll open a few memories from the jar and read them together.

You might light a candle, play a favorite song, or cook a dish your loved one enjoyed. The goal is continuity, not perfection.

Step 5: Supporting Each Other Beyond the Ritual

As you share, notice emotional differences:

Some may cry while others stay quiet.

Some may laugh while others sit in silence.

All are valid.

End the ritual by asking, "What can we do this week to take care of one another?"

Agree on one small act of kindness or check-in for the days ahead.

Reflection Prompt:

"How does sharing memories together change the way I feel about my own grief? What have I learned about how my family loves and heals?"

References

American Psychiatric Association. (2013). Diagnostic and statistical manual of mental disorders (5th ed.). Arlington, VA: American Psychiatric Publishing.

Berger, R., & McLeod, J. (2006). Incorporating nature into therapy: A framework for practice. Journal of Systemic Therapies, 25(2), 80-94.

Hilliard, R. E. (2001). The effects of music therapy-based bereavement groups on mood and behavior of grieving children: A pilot study. Journal of Music Therapy, 38(4), 291-306.

Levy, F. J. (1988). Dance/movement therapy: A healing art. Reston, VA: American Alliance for Health, Physical Education, Recreation and Dance.

Malchiodi, C. A. (2012). Handbook of art therapy. New York, NY: Guilford Press.

Neimeyer, R. A., & Currier, J. M. (2009). Grief therapy: Evidence of efficacy and emerging directions. Current Directions in Psychological Science, 18(6), 352-356.

Pennebaker, J. W., & Seagal, J. D. (1999). Forming a story: The health benefits of narrative. Journal of Clinical Psychology, 55(10), 1243-1254.

Shear, M. K. (2015). Complicated grief. New England Journal of Medicine, 372(2), 153-160.

Chapter 8

Tears Are Not a Sign of Weakness

The Importance of Allowing Yourself to Grieve

Grief is a deeply personal and often messy process. It defies timelines, expectations, and societal norms. Yet, one of the most universal aspects of grief is the act of crying. Tears are a natural and necessary response to loss, yet many people feel pressured to suppress them, fearing judgment or appearing weak.

The Healing Power of Crying

Why Tears Are Necessary

Crying is one of the most primal and human responses to pain. It is a physical manifestation of emotional release, a way for the body to process and cope with overwhelming feelings. While society often views crying as a sign of vulnerability or weakness, research suggests that tears serve an important biological and psychological function.

The Science Behind Tears

Tears come in different forms. Basal tears keep eyes lubricated, reflex tears wash out irritants, and emotional tears appear when we experience strong feelings (Vingerhoets, 2013). Emotional tears contain stress hormones like cortisol, and shedding them may help the body regulate stress (Gračanin, Bylsma, & Vingerhoets, 2014).

Emotional Benefits of Crying

Crying is not just a physical release; it also has profound psychological benefits. Studies have shown that crying can:

Reduce Stress: Crying activates the parasympathetic nervous system, which helps the body relax and recover from stress (Gračanin et al., 2014).

Improve Mood: While crying may initially feel painful, it often leads to a sense of catharsis and emotional relief. Many people report feeling lighter and more at peace after a good cry (Rottenberg, Bylsma, & Vingerhoets, 2008).

Foster Connection: Crying can signal to others that we need support, fostering empathy and connection. In this way, tears can strengthen relationships and create a sense of community (Vingerhoets, 2013).

Promote Emotional Processing: Crying allows us to confront and process difficult emotions, which is a crucial step in the grieving process (Kennedy-Moore & Watson, 2001).

Despite these benefits, many people feel ashamed or embarrassed to cry, especially in public. This reluctance often stems from societal expectations and cultural norms that discourage emotional expression.

Society's Expectations Why We're Taught to Hide Our Grief

From a young age, many of us are taught to suppress our emotions. Boys, in particular, are often told to "be strong" and "not cry," while girls may be encouraged to hide their tears to avoid appearing overly emotional. These messages are reinforced by societal norms that equate emotional expression with weakness or instability.

The Stigma of Grief

Grief, in particular, is often stigmatized. In many cultures, there is an unspoken expectation that individuals should "move on" or "get over" their loss within a certain timeframe. This pressure can lead to what psychologist Kenneth Doka calls "disenfranchised grief," where a person's grief is not acknowledged or validated by society (Doka, 2002). Disenfranchised grief can occur when the loss is not recognized as significant (e.g., the death of a pet), when the relationship is not acknowledged (e.g., a secret lover), or when the griever is not seen as capable of grieving (e.g., a child or someone with cognitive impairments).

The Impact of Suppressing Grief

Suppressing grief can have serious consequences for both mental and physical health. Research has shown that individuals who inhibit their emotions are more likely to experience anxiety, depression, and even physical illnesses such as cardiovascular disease (Pennebaker & Beall, 1986). In contrast, allowing oneself to grieve openly can lead to greater emotional resilience and well-being (Stroebe, Schut, & Stroebe, 2007).

Challenging Societal Norms

To create a more compassionate and understanding society, it is essential to challenge the norms that discourage emotional expression. This begins with recognizing that grief is a natural and necessary response to loss, and that tears are not a sign of weakness but a testament to the depth of our love and connection.

Creating Safe Spaces

How to Grieve Authentically Without Judgment

For many people, the fear of judgment or rejection can make it difficult to grieve openly. Creating safe spaces both internally and externally where grief can be expressed authentically is crucial for healing.

Internal Safe Spaces

An internal safe space is a mental and emotional environment where you allow yourself to feel and express your grief without self-judgment. Here are some ways to cultivate this:

Practice Self-Compassion: Treat yourself with the same kindness and understanding you would offer to a friend.

Acknowledge that grief is a difficult process and that it's okay to feel sad, angry, or confused.

Challenge Negative Self-Talk: Replace self-critical thoughts like "I should be over this by now" with more compassionate ones, such as "It's okay to take my time."

Set Boundaries: Protect your emotional energy by setting boundaries with people or situations that feel draining or unsupportive.

External Safe Spaces

An external safe space is a physical or social environment where you feel comfortable expressing your grief. Here are some ways to create or find such spaces:

Seek Supportive Relationships: Surround yourself with people who validate your feelings and offer empathy rather than judgment. This might include friends, family, or a grief support group.

Create a Grief Ritual: Designate a time and place where you can grieve freely, whether it's a quiet corner of your home or a special spot in nature.

Use Creative Outlets: Art, music, and writing can provide a safe and non-judgmental way to express your emotions.

Consider Therapy: A therapist can provide a safe and confidential space to explore your grief and develop coping strategies.

The Role of Community

Creating safe spaces is not just an individual responsibility; it is also a collective one. Communities can play a vital role in normalizing grief and providing support. This might involve:

Educating Others: Raising awareness about the importance of emotional expression and the healing power of tears.

Offering Support: Creating grief support groups or community rituals that honor loss.

Challenging Stigma: Speaking out against societal norms that discourage emotional expression.

By creating safe spaces both within ourselves and in our communities we can foster a culture of compassion and understanding that allows grief to be experienced authentically and without judgment.

The Importance of Self-Compassion in Grief

One of the most challenging aspects of grief is the emotional toll it takes on an individual. Feelings of guilt, regret, and self-blame are common, and they can exacerbate the pain of loss. Practicing self-compassion treating oneself with the same kindness and understanding that one might offer to a close friend can be a powerful tool in the healing process.

What Is Self-Compassion?

Self-compassion, as defined by Dr. Kristin Neff, involves three core components: self-kindness, common humanity, and mindfulness (Neff, 2003).

Self-Kindness: This involves being gentle and understanding with oneself rather than harshly self-critical. For example, instead of berating yourself for not "moving on" quickly enough, you might acknowledge that grief is a difficult process and that it’s okay to take your time.

Common Humanity: Recognizing that suffering and loss are universal human experiences can help alleviate feelings of isolation. Understanding that others have walked a similar path can provide comfort and a sense of connection.

Mindfulness: This involves being present with your emotions without judgment or avoidance. It means allowing yourself to feel the pain of grief without trying to suppress or deny it.

How Self-Compassion Helps in Grief

Research has shown that self-compassion can reduce symptoms of depression and anxiety, which are often associated with grief (Neff, 2011). By treating yourself with kindness and understanding, you create a safe internal environment where healing can occur. Self-compassion also helps to counteract the negative self-talk that often accompanies grief, such as thoughts like "I should have done more" or "I don't deserve to be happy."

Practicing Self-Compassion

Here are some practical ways to cultivate self-compassion during the grieving process:

Write a Self-Compassion Letter: Write a letter to yourself from the perspective of a compassionate friend. Acknowledge your pain, validate your feelings, and offer words of comfort and encouragement.

Practice Self-Compassion Breaks: When you notice yourself feeling overwhelmed by grief, take a moment to pause. Place your hand over your heart, take a deep breath, and offer yourself kind words, such as "This is really hard right now, but I'm doing the best I can."

Challenge Negative Self-Talk: When you catch yourself engaging in self-critical thoughts, ask yourself, "Would I say this to a friend?" If the answer is no, reframe the thought in a more compassionate way.

Engage in Self-Care Rituals: Treat yourself with the same care you would offer to a loved one. This might include taking a warm bath, going for a walk in nature, or simply allowing yourself to rest.

By practicing self-compassion, you can create a more nurturing and supportive relationship with yourself, which can help ease the pain of grief and foster resilience.

The Role of Rituals in Grief

Rituals have long been used as a way to honor the dead and provide structure to the grieving process. Whether they are cultural, religious, or personal, rituals can offer a sense of meaning and continuity in the face of loss.

Why Rituals Matter

Rituals serve several important functions in grief:

Providing Structure: Grief can feel chaotic and overwhelming. Rituals offer a sense of order and predictability, which can be comforting during a time of upheaval.

Honoring the Deceased: Rituals allow individuals to express their love and respect for the person who has died. This can be a meaningful way to keep their memory alive.

Facilitating Emotional Expression: Rituals provide a safe space to express emotions, whether through tears, prayers, or shared stories.

Creating Connection: Rituals often involve family and community, fostering a sense of connection and support.

Examples of Grief Rituals

Rituals can take many forms, depending on cultural, religious, and personal preferences. Here are some examples:

Memorial Services: Holding a memorial service or celebration of life can provide an opportunity for family and friends to come together and honor the deceased.

Lighting a Candle: Lighting a candle in memory of a loved one can be a simple yet powerful ritual. It can be done daily, on special occasions, or whenever you feel the need to connect with their memory.

Creating a Memory Box: A memory box can hold items that remind you of your loved one, such as photographs, letters, or personal belongings. You can add to it over time and revisit it whenever you want to feel close to them.

Writing Letters: Writing letters to the deceased can be a way to express unresolved feelings, share updates, or simply feel connected to them.

Planting a Tree or Garden: Planting a tree or creating a garden in memory of a loved one can serve as a living tribute and a source of comfort.

Annual Remembrances: Marking the anniversary of a loved one's death or their birthday with a special ritual can help keep their memory alive.

Rituals are deeply personal, and there is no right or wrong way to create them. The key is to choose rituals that feel meaningful and comforting to you.

The Power of Connection in Grief

Grief can be an isolating experience, but connection whether with friends, family, or a broader community can be a powerful antidote to loneliness. Building and maintaining connections during grief can provide emotional support, practical assistance, and a sense of belonging.

Reaching Out to Loved Ones

It's common for grieving individuals to withdraw from social interactions, either because they feel overwhelmed or because they fear burdening others. However, reaching out to loved ones can be an important step in the healing process. Here are some ways to stay connected:

Share Your Feelings: Let trusted friends or family members know how you're feeling. You don't have to go through grief alone.

Ask for Help: Grief can make even simple tasks feel daunting. Don't hesitate to ask for help with practical matters, such as cooking, cleaning, or running errands.

Stay Engaged: Even if you don't feel like socializing, try to stay engaged with your community. This might involve attending a support group, joining a club, or participating in a hobby.

Building New Connections

In addition to maintaining existing relationships, building new connections can also be beneficial. This might involve:

Joining a Support Group: As discussed earlier, support groups provide a sense of community and understanding. They can be a valuable source of connection and support.

Volunteering: Volunteering for a cause that was important to your loved one can be a meaningful way to honor their memory and connect with others who share your values.

Exploring New Interests: Grief can sometimes lead to a reevaluation of priorities. Exploring new interests or hobbies can provide a sense of purpose and help you meet new people.

The Role of Technology in Connection

In today's digital age, technology can also play a role in fostering connection. Online support groups, social media, and video calls can help people stay connected with loved ones, even when physical distance is a barrier.

The Journey Toward Meaning-Making

One of the most profound aspects of grief is the search for meaning. In the wake of loss, many individuals grapple with existential questions, such as "Why did this happen?" or "What is the purpose of life?" While these questions may not have clear answers, the process of meaning-making can be an important part of the healing journey.

What Is Meaning-Making?

Meaning-making refers to the process of finding or creating meaning in the face of loss. This might involve:

Finding Purpose: Some individuals find meaning by channeling their grief into a cause or activity that honors their loved one. For example, a parent who has lost a child might start a foundation to support other families in similar situations.

Reframing the Loss: Reframing involves looking at the loss from a different perspective. This might involve focusing on the positive memories and lessons learned from the relationship, rather than solely on the pain of the loss.

Spiritual or Philosophical Exploration: For some, meaning-making involves exploring spiritual or philosophical beliefs about life, death, and the afterlife.

The Role of Legacy

Creating a legacy for your loved one can also be a powerful way to find meaning. This might involve:

Sharing Their Story: Keeping your loved one's memory alive by sharing their story with others can be a meaningful way to honor their life.

Continuing Their Work: If your loved one was passionate about a particular cause, continuing their work can be a way to carry on their legacy.

Creating Art or Writing: Creating art, music, or writing in memory of your loved one can be a way to express your grief and keep their memory alive.

Conclusion

Navigating the pain of grief is a complex and deeply personal journey. Whether you are experiencing complicated grief, seeking therapy, or exploring creative outlets, there are many paths to healing. By practicing self-compassion, engaging in meaningful rituals, fostering connections, and exploring the search for meaning, you can begin to move through the pain of loss and find a way forward.

Grief is not something to be "fixed" or "overcome," but rather a process to be lived through. It is a testament to the love and connection we shared with those we have lost. By honoring your grief and taking steps to care for yourself, you can find a way to carry your loss with you while still embracing life.

Exercise: The Permission to Feel Journal

Purpose:

To release the internal pressure to "stay strong" and to reconnect with the natural healing that comes from letting tears and emotions flow freely.

Materials Needed:

A quiet space where you can be alone

A notebook or journal

Tissues (and compassion for yourself)

Step 1: Create a Safe Container for Emotion

Find a private, peaceful setting—somewhere you can cry, write, or sit quietly without interruption.

Begin by taking a few slow breaths. Tell yourself:

"I'm safe to feel what I feel. My emotions are not my enemies."

If it helps, light a candle or play calming music to set a tone of comfort and safety.

Step 2: Write Without Censoring

In your journal, respond to these prompts:

1. What do I most want to say but haven't allowed myself to?
2. When did I first start believing that crying was weakness?
3. What happens in my body when I fight back tears?
4. What happens when I allow them?

Write freely, don't worry about grammar, spelling, or length. The goal is honesty, not perfection.

Step 3: Reframe Strength

After journaling, read your words back slowly.

Underline any phrases that reveal self-blame or shame about being emotional. Then, next to each, write a gentle truth to replace it.

Examples:

"Crying makes me weak" → "Crying shows my humanity."

"I should have moved on by now" → "Healing takes the time it takes."

"I'm tired of feeling sad" → "Sadness is part of remembering love."

Step 4: The Emotional Release Practice

If tears come, let them. If they don't, that's okay too. Sit quietly and notice what your body feels: tightness, warmth, heaviness, calm.

You might place a hand over your heart and say aloud:

"This is what love looks like when it hurts. And that's okay."

Step 5: Closing Reflection

When you're ready, write one closing sentence that honors your strength in being open:

"Today I gave myself permission to feel, and that is enough."

Consider marking this page with a ribbon or star so you can revisit it whenever you start to hold back again.

Reflection Prompt:

"What would it mean to see my tears as proof of love rather than weakness?"

References

Bonanno, G. A. (2009). The other side of sadness: What the new science of bereavement tells us about life after loss. Basic Books.

Butler, E. A., Gross, J. J., & Barnard, K. (2003). Emotion regulation and relationship functioning: Physiological, cognitive, and behavioral consequences of suppression. Journal of Personality and Social Psychology, 85(2), 312–327.

Doka, K. J. (2002). Disenfranchised grief: Recognizing hidden sorrow. Lexington Books.

Gračanin, A., Bylsma, L. M., & Vingerhoets, A. J. J. M. (2014). Is crying a self-soothing behavior? Frontiers in Psychology, 5, 502.

Gross, J. J., & John, O. P. (2003). Individual differences in two emotion regulation processes: Implications for affect, relationships, and well-being. Journal of Personality and Social Psychology, 85(2), 348–362.

Kennedy-Moore, E., & Watson, J. C. (2001). How and when does emotional expression help? Review of General Psychology, 5(3), 187–212.

Klass, D., Silverman, P. R., & Nickman, S. L. (Eds.). (1996). Continuing bonds: New understandings of grief. Taylor & Francis.

Neff, K. D. (2003). Self-compassion: An alternative conceptualization of a healthy attitude toward oneself. Self and Identity, 2(2), 85–101.

Neff, K. D., & Germer, C. K. (2013). A pilot study and randomized controlled trial of the mindful self-compassion program. Journal of Clinical Psychology, 69(1), 28–44.

Park, C. L. (2010). Making sense of the meaning literature: An integrative review of meaning making and its effects on adjustment to stressful life events. Psychological Bulletin, 136(2), 257–301.

Pennebaker, J. W., & Beall, S. K. (1986). Confronting a traumatic event: Toward an understanding of inhibition and disease. Journal of Abnormal Psychology, 95(3), 274–281.

Rottenberg, J., Bylsma, L. M., & Vingerhoets, A. J. J. M. (2008). Is crying beneficial? Current Directions in Psychological Science, 17(6), 400–404.

Stroebe, M., Schut, H., & Stroebe, W. (2007). Health outcomes of bereavement. The Lancet, 370(9603), 1960–1973.

Vingerhoets, A. J. J. M. (2013). Why only humans weep: Unravelling the mysteries of tears. Oxford University Press.

Walter, T. (2015). Communication media and the dead: From the stone age to Facebook. Mortality, 20(3), 215–232.

Worden, J. W. (2018). Grief counseling and grief therapy: A handbook for the mental health practitioner (5th ed.). Springer Publishing Company.

Chapter 9

The Things They Left Behind

How Physical Reminders Bring Both Comfort and Pain

After the death of a loved one, their possessions often become a source of both comfort and pain. Clothing, jewelry, photographs, and other keepsakes serve as tangible reminders of the person we have lost, evoking memories and emotions that can be both soothing and overwhelming.

The Weight of Objects

Clothing, Jewelry, and Other Keepsakes

Physical objects can evoke powerful memories. A favorite sweater, a piece of jewelry, or a handwritten note can transport us back to moments shared with someone we've lost. These items often provide a sense of comfort, connecting past and present (Vingerhoets, 2013).

The Emotional Significance of Objects

Objects hold meaning because of the memories and emotions attached to them (Kennedy-Moore & Watson, 2001). For example:

Clothing: A loved one's clothing may carry their scent, evoking a sense of their presence. Wearing their favorite sweater or holding their scarf can provide a sense of closeness and comfort.

Jewelry: A piece of jewelry, such as a wedding ring or a necklace, may symbolize a special bond or shared experience. Wearing or holding the jewelry can serve as a reminder of that connection.

Photographs: Photographs capture moments in time, preserving memories that might otherwise fade. Looking at photos can evoke a range of emotions, from joy and gratitude to sadness and longing.

Everyday Items: Even mundane objects, such as a coffee mug or a book, can hold deep emotional significance if they were meaningful to the deceased.

The Dual Nature of Objects

Objects can comfort and hurt. The same sweater that feels like a hug might also remind us of loss. This duality is a common part of grief, where the same object can evoke both comfort and sorrow (Gračanin, Bylsma, & Vingerhoets, 2014).

The Paradox of Possessions

When Holding On Hurts More Than It Helps

For some, holding on to a loved one's possessions can become a source of distress. The desire to preserve their memory may clash with the pain of being constantly reminded of their absence. This paradox can make it difficult to decide what to keep, what to let go of, and when (Doka, 2002).

The Challenges of Letting Go

Letting go of a loved one's possessions can feel like letting go of a part of them. This can be especially difficult if the objects are tied to significant memories or if they represent the last tangible connection to the deceased. However, holding on to too many possessions can also create emotional clutter, making it harder to move forward (Pennebaker & Beall, 1986).

Finding Balance

Finding a balance between holding on and letting go is a deeply personal process. Here are some strategies to consider:

Take Your Time: There is no rush to sort through a loved one's belongings. Give yourself permission to take as much time as you need.

Prioritize Meaningful Items: Focus on keeping items that hold the most emotional significance. Letting go of less meaningful possessions can create space for the ones that truly matter.

Involve Others: Sorting through possessions can be overwhelming. Consider asking a trusted friend or family member to help.

Create a Ritual: Letting go of possessions can be a meaningful act of closure. Consider creating a ritual, such as donating items to a charity or giving them to someone who will appreciate them.

Honor Their Legacy: Letting go of possessions does not mean letting go of memories. Find other ways to honor your loved one's legacy, such as creating a memory box or planting a tree in their honor.

Creating a Memory Box

A Tangible Way to Honor Their Legacy

A memory box is a tangible way to preserve and honor a loved one's legacy. It can serve as a safe space to store meaningful objects, photographs, and mementos, allowing you to revisit memories when you are ready.

How to Create a Memory Box

Choose a Container: Select a box or container that feels special. This could be a decorative box, a wooden chest, or even a simple shoebox.

Gather Items: Collect items that hold emotional significance, such as photographs, letters, jewelry, or small keepsakes.

Add Personal Touches: Consider adding personal touches, such as a handwritten note, a poem, or a drawing.

Store in a Safe Place: Keep the memory box in a safe and accessible place where you can revisit it whenever you need comfort or connection.

The Benefits of a Memory Box

A memory box can provide a sense of continuity and connection, serving as a tangible reminder of the love and memories you shared. It can also be a helpful tool for processing grief, allowing you to revisit memories at your own pace.

Conclusion

Grief is a complex and multifaceted journey, and the way we navigate it is deeply personal. Whether through tears, physical objects, or memory boxes, finding ways to honor and process our grief is essential for healing. By allowing ourselves to grieve authentically and creating spaces both physical and emotional where grief can be expressed without judgment, we can begin to move through the pain and find a way forward.

Exercise: The Three Types of Tears Reflection

Purpose:

To help you understand the physical and emotional role of tears, and to use that awareness as part of your self-healing process.

Materials Needed:

Journal or notebook

Pen or pencil

A quiet place to sit and reflect

Step 1: Learn the Language of Tears

There are three main types of tears:

1. Basal tears – keep your eyes moist and healthy.

2. Reflex tears – protect you from irritants like smoke or dust.

3. Emotional tears – carry stress hormones and toxins from the body and signal emotional release.

Think about that last one—your body is designed to help you grieve. Crying isn't a failure; it's your biology supporting emotional survival.

Step 2: Reflect on Your Relationship with Crying

In your journal, write or think about:

When was the last time I cried, and what triggered it?

How did I feel before, during, and after?

Have I ever felt ashamed or pressured not to cry? Who or what shaped that belief?

What would change if I allowed tears more freely?

Be honest—there are no wrong answers.

Step 3: Practice the Release

If you feel tears coming, allow them without resistance.

If not, place your hand over your chest and take slow breaths. Whisper softly:

"I'm letting go of what my body no longer needs to hold."

Even without tears, that act of mindfulness calms the nervous system and signals safety to the brain.

Step 4: Record the Aftermath

After the moment passes, write down:

What emotions came up?

Did you notice any physical change (relaxation, warmth, fatigue, peace)?

What memory or thought surfaced?

Over time, you'll start to see how crying helps your body complete emotional cycles.

Step 5: Create a Gentle Reminder

Write one of these affirmations somewhere visible—or create your own:

"Tears are proof that I'm healing."

"My body knows how to release pain."

"Each tear carries a story that deserves to be heard."

Reflection Prompt:

"What happens when I stop trying to control my tears and instead let them teach me what needs attention?"

References

Doka, K. J. (2002). Disenfranchised grief: New directions, challenges, and strategies for practice. Champaign, IL: Research Press.

Gračanin, A., Bylsma, L. M., & Vingerhoets, A. J. J. M. (2014). Is crying a self-soothing behavior? Frontiers in Psychology, 5, 502.

Kennedy-Moore, E., & Watson, J. C. (2001). Expressing emotion: Myths, realities, and therapeutic strategies. New York, NY: Guilford Press.

Pennebaker, J. W., & Beall, S. K. (1986). Confronting a traumatic event: Toward an understanding of inhibition and disease. Journal of Abnormal Psychology, 95(3), 274-281.

Rottenberg, J., Bylsma, L. M., & Vingerhoets, A. J. J. M. (2008). Is crying beneficial? Current Directions in Psychological Science, 17(6), 400-404.

Stroebe, M., Schut, H., & Stroebe, W. (2007). Health outcomes of bereavement. The Lancet, 370(9603), 1960-1973.

Vingerhoets, A. J. J. M. (2013). Why only humans weep: Unravelling the mysteries of tears. Oxford, UK: Oxford University Press.

Chapter 10

When the World Moves On

Dealing with the Feeling That Others Forget Too Soon

Grief is a deeply personal journey, one that unfolds at its own pace and in its own way. Yet, as time passes, the world around you continues to move forward, often at a pace that feels jarring and incongruent with your own experience. This dissonance can lead to feelings of isolation, frustration, and even anger.

The Isolation of Grief

Why Others Seem to Move On Faster

One of the most painful aspects of grief is the sense of isolation that often accompanies it. While your world has been irrevocably altered by loss, the lives of those around you continue seemingly unchanged. Friends, family, and colleagues may offer their condolences initially, but as weeks and months pass, their attention shifts back to their own lives. This can leave you feeling as though your grief is invisible, or worse, that others have forgotten your loss altogether.

The Psychology of Grief and Social Isolation

Grief is inherently isolating because it is an internal experience that others cannot fully see or understand. As Neimeyer, Burke, Mackay, and van Dyke Stringer (2010) note, grief disrupts the assumptive world of the bereaved, creating a sense of disconnection from others who have not experienced the same loss. This disconnection can be exacerbated by societal norms that discourage open expressions of grief, particularly after the initial period of mourning has passed (Stroebe, Schut, & Stroebe, 2007).

Moreover, the pace at which others seem to "move on" can feel dismissive of your pain. However, it is important to recognize that this perception may not reflect reality. Others may not have forgotten your loss; rather, they may be unsure of how to support you or may fear saying the wrong thing. As Doka (2008) notes, societal discomfort with grief often leads to a phenomenon known as "disenfranchised grief," where the bereaved feel that their loss is not acknowledged or validated by others.

Story

The Six-Month Mark

Six months after the funeral, people stopped asking how she was doing.

At work, conversations returned to normal topics. Invitations resumed. Someone even said, kindly but casually, "It's good to see you getting back to yourself."

She smiled politely, but inside she wondered what version of herself they believed had returned. The life she had known was still gone.

Coping with the Isolation

To navigate the isolation of grief, it is essential to acknowledge and validate your own feelings. Allow yourself to grieve at your own pace, without comparing your journey to that of others. Seek out individuals who are willing to listen without judgment, even if they cannot fully understand your experience. Additionally, consider joining a grief support group, where you can connect with others who are navigating similar emotions (Worden, 2018).

Navigating Anniversaries and Milestones

When the World Doesn't Remember

Anniversaries, birthdays, and other milestones can be particularly challenging for those who are grieving. These dates serve as poignant reminders of the loss, yet the world around you may not acknowledge them. This lack of recognition can intensify feelings of loneliness and sadness, as though the significance of your loss has been forgotten.

The Impact of Unacknowledged Milestones

Research has shown that anniversaries and other significant dates can trigger a resurgence of grief, often referred to as the "anniversary reaction" (Carnelley, Wortman, & Kessler, 1999). This reaction can manifest as heightened sadness, anxiety, or even physical symptoms. When these milestones go unacknowledged by others, it can feel as though your grief is being invalidated, compounding the emotional pain.

For example, the first anniversary of a loved one's death may be a day of profound significance for you, yet others may not remember the date or may assume that you have "moved on." This discrepancy between your internal experience and the external world can create a perception of alienation.

Honoring Your Loved One in Meaningful Ways

To navigate these challenging moments, consider creating personal rituals or traditions that honor your loved one's memory. This might involve lighting a candle, visiting a special place, or writing a letter to the person you have lost. These acts can provide a feeling of connection and continuity, even when others do not acknowledge the significance of the date (Neimeyer, 2012).

Additionally, communicate your needs to those close to you. Let them know that certain dates are important to you and that their support during these times would be meaningful. While they may not fully understand your experience, most people are willing to offer support when they know how to do so (Klass, Silverman, & Nickman, 1996).

Finding Your Tribe

Connecting with Others Who Understand Your Pain

One of the most powerful antidotes to the isolation of grief is finding a community of individuals who share your experience. These connections can provide validation, understanding, and a feeling of belonging that is often lacking in other relationships.

The Importance of Shared Experience

Grief support groups, whether in-person or online, offer a space where you can share your story and hear the stories of others who have experienced similar losses. This shared experience can be profoundly healing, as it reminds you that you are not alone in your pain. As Yalom and Leszcz (2005) describe, group therapy provides a sense of universality, helping individuals realize that their feelings are normal and shared by others.

In addition to formal support groups, consider seeking out communities that align with your specific type of loss. For example, there are organizations dedicated to supporting parents who have lost children, individuals who have lost spouses, and those who have experienced traumatic losses. These communities can offer specialized resources and understanding that may not be available in more general groups.

Building Meaningful Connections

When seeking out a grief community, it is important to find a group that feels like the right fit for you. Attend a few meetings or participate in online forums to get an impression of the group's dynamics and whether it aligns with your needs. Look for a community that fosters empathy, respect, and open communication.

In addition to formal support groups, consider reaching out to individuals in your personal network who have experienced loss. These one-on-one connections can provide a deeper level of understanding and support. As Tedeschi and Calhoun (2004) note, finding meaning in grief often involves connecting with others who can offer perspective and hope.

The Role of Professional Support

While peer support is invaluable, it is also important to recognize when professional help may be needed. Grief counselors and therapists can provide guidance and tools for navigating the complex emotions of loss. They can also help you process feelings of isolation and develop strategies for reconnecting with the world around you (Shear, 2012).

Conclusion

The journey through grief is rarely linear, and the feeling that others have moved on too soon can add an additional layer of pain to an already difficult experience. By acknowledging the isolation of grief, honoring significant milestones in meaningful ways, and finding a community that understands your pain, you can begin to navigate this challenging terrain with greater resilience and hope.

Remember, your grief is a testament to the love and connection you shared with the person you have lost. While the world may move on, your journey is uniquely your own, and it is okay to take the time you need to heal. In finding your tribe, you can discover belonging and understanding that helps to light the path forward.

Exercise: Reclaiming Your Space in a World That's Moved On

Purpose:

To help you acknowledge your grief without resentment toward others who may have returned to "normal life," and to build healthy ways of staying connected to your loved one while also moving at your own pace.

Step 1: The Circle of Awareness

Draw two overlapping circles on a blank page. Label one "My Grief" and the other "The World."

In the "My Grief" circle, write words or phrases that describe how you feel today — lonely, forgotten, grateful, angry, or any other emotions that surface.

In the "The World" circle, list what you notice around you — people returning to routines, events you feel disconnected from, or expectations that seem hard to meet.

In the overlapping space, note moments where you still connect with the world — a friend who checks in, a song that reminds you of your loved one, or a quiet moment of peace.

Take a few minutes to reflect: Where am I resisting connection? Where am I ready to re-engage, even a little?

Step 2: Memory Anchors

Choose one small way to honor your loved one this week that feels private and meaningful — lighting a candle, wearing something that reminds you of them, visiting a place they loved, or doing a kind act in their name.

Write down how it makes you feel before and after. The goal isn't to erase pain, but to remind yourself that remembrance doesn't depend on others remembering too.

Step 3: Finding Your Tribe

Make a short list of people or spaces where your grief feels understood — a friend, a support group, a spiritual leader, or even an online community.

If you don't have one yet, list where you might start looking: local bereavement groups, community centers, or grief-focused podcasts.

Then, set a simple intention: "I will reach out to one supportive space this week."

Reflection Prompt:

Write a short journal entry titled "The World Keeps Turning, But So Do I."

Describe what it feels like to live in a world that has moved on and what small steps you're taking to move forward without leaving your loved one behind.

References

Carnelley, K. B., Wortman, C. B., & Kessler, R. C. (1999). The impact of widowhood on depression: Findings from a prospective survey. Psychological Medicine, 29(5), 1111-1123.

Doka, K. J. (2008). Disenfranchised grief in historical and cultural perspective. In M. S. Stroebe, R. O. Hansson, H. Schut, & W. Stroebe (Eds.), Handbook of bereavement research and practice: Advances in theory and intervention (pp. 223-240). American Psychological Association.

Klass, D., Silverman, P. R., & Nickman, S. L. (1996). Continuing bonds: New understandings of grief. Taylor & Francis.

Neimeyer, R. A. (2012). Techniques of grief therapy: Creative practices for counseling the bereaved. Routledge.

Neimeyer, R. A., Burke, L. A., Mackay, M. M., & van Dyke Stringer, J. G. (2010). Grief therapy and the reconstruction of meaning: From principles to practice. Journal of Contemporary Psychotherapy, 40(2), 73-83.

Shear, M. K. (2012). Grief and mourning gone awry: Pathway and course of complicated grief. Dialogues in Clinical Neuroscience, 14(2), 119-128.

Stroebe, M., Schut, H., & Stroebe, W. (2007). Health outcomes of bereavement. The Lancet, 370(9603), 1960-1973

Tedeschi, R. G., & Calhoun, L. G. (2004). Posttraumatic growth: Conceptual foundations and empirical evidence. Psychological Inquiry, 15(1), 1-18.

Worden, J. W. (2018). Grief counseling and grief therapy: A handbook for the mental health practitioner (5th ed.). Springer Publishing Company.

Yalom, I. D., & Leszcz, M. (2005). The theory and practice of group psychotherapy (5th ed.). Basic Books.

Part 3: Finding Light in the Darkness

Chapter 11

Love Never Dies

Holding On to Memories While Moving Forward

Grief is not a journey that ends with "closure." Instead, it is a lifelong relationship with loss, memory, and love. As you navigate the complexities of grief, you may find yourself grappling with how to honor the past while moving forward into the future. Although death changes the form of our relationships, it does not erase the love that created them. The bonds we share with those we lose continue to shape our lives in quiet and lasting ways.

The Role of Memory in Healing

How to Cherish the Past Without Being Stuck in It

Memories are the threads that connect us to those we have lost. They are the echoes of laughter, the warmth of a shared moment, and the imprint of a loved one's presence in our lives. Yet, memories can also be a double-edged sword. While they provide comfort and connection, they can also keep us tethered to the past, making it difficult to move forward.

The Dual Nature of Memory in Grief

Memory plays a central role in the grieving process. According to Neimeyer (2012), memories help us reconstruct our relationship with the deceased, allowing us to integrate the loss into our ongoing life narrative. However, when memories become a source of rumination or avoidance, they can hinder healing. For example, constantly replaying the final moments of a loved one's life may lead to prolonged grief, while avoiding memories altogether can prevent the necessary processing of loss (Boelen, van den Hout, & van den Bout, 2006).

The key is to find a balance cherishing the past without being trapped by it. This involves actively engaging with memories in a way that fosters meaning and connection, rather than pain and stagnation.

Strategies for Healthy Engagement with Memory

Create a Memory Ritual: Designate a specific time or activity to honor your loved one's memory. This could be lighting a candle on their birthday, visiting a place that was meaningful to them, or writing a letter expressing your thoughts and feelings. Rituals provide structure and intentionality, allowing you to engage with memories in a way that feels purposeful (Romanoff & Terenzio, 1998).

Use Memory Triggers as Opportunities for Reflection: Certain sights, sounds, or smells may trigger memories of your loved one. Instead of avoiding these triggers, use them as opportunities to reflect on the positive aspects of your relationship. For example, if a particular song reminds you of them, take a moment to listen and recall the joy it brought to both of you.

Practice Mindfulness: Mindfulness techniques can help you stay present while engaging with memories. When a memory arises, acknowledge it without judgment, allowing yourself to experience the emotions it evokes without becoming overwhelmed (Kabat-Zinn, 2003).

Stories That Keep Them Alive

Sharing Memories with Others

One of the most powerful ways to keep a loved one's memory alive is through storytelling. Sharing stories not only preserves their legacy but also creates connection and continuity. When you share memories with others, you invite them to participate in the ongoing narrative of your loved one's life.

The Healing Power of Storytelling

Storytelling is a universal human experience that transcends cultures and generations. It allows us to make sense of our experiences, process emotions, and create meaning (Pennebaker & Seagal, 1999). In the context of grief, sharing stories about a loved one can help you feel closer to them and provide comfort and validation.

For example, sharing a funny story or remembering a cherished moment can spark joy and renew the feeling of connection, even during sadness. It also allows others to see your loved one through your eyes, fostering a deeper understanding of their impact on your life.

How to Share Memories Effectively

Create a Memory Book or Journal: Compile photos, letters, and stories in a memory book or journal. This can serve as a tangible keepsake that you can revisit and share with others. Encourage family and friends to contribute their own memories, creating a collective tribute to your loved one.

Host a Memory-Sharing Gathering: Organize a gathering where friends and family can come together to share stories and memories. This could be a formal event, such as a memorial service, or an informal gathering, such as a dinner or picnic. The act of coming together to remember can be deeply healing.

Use Technology to Preserve Memories: In today's digital age, there are countless ways to preserve and share memories online. Create a memorial website, a social media page, or a video tribute that can be accessed by others. These platforms allow you to reach a wider audience and create a lasting legacy.

The Legacy of Love

How Their Impact Continues to Shape Your Life

The love you shared with your loved one does not end with their death. Instead, it becomes a part of who you are, shaping your values, actions, and relationships. This enduring legacy is a testament to the profound impact they had on your life.

Understanding the Concept of Legacy

Legacy is not just about material possessions or achievements; it is about the intangible qualities that define a person's essence. It is the kindness they showed, the lessons they taught, and the love they shared. As Klass, Silverman, and Nickman (1996) detail the concept of "continuing bonds," emphasizing the ongoing relationship between the bereaved and the deceased, even after death.

Your loved one's legacy lives on through the ways they influenced you and the world around them. By recognizing and honoring this legacy, you can find meaning and purpose in your grief.

Ways to Honor Their Legacy

Live Their Values: Reflect on the values and principles that were important to your loved one. Consider how you can incorporate these values into your own life. For example, if they were passionate about helping others, you might volunteer for a cause they cared about.

Create a Legacy Project: A legacy project is a tangible way to honor your loved one's memory and impact. This could be a scholarship fund, a community garden, or a charitable organization in their name. The project serves as a living tribute that continues to make a difference in the world.

Pass On Their Wisdom: Share the lessons and wisdom your loved one imparted to you with others. Whether it's through storytelling, mentoring, or teaching, passing on their knowledge ensures that their influence continues to grow.

Celebrate Their Life: Find ways to celebrate your loved one's life and the joy they brought to others. This could be through an annual event, a creative project, or simply by living a life that reflects their spirit.

Exercise: Keeping the Connection Alive

Purpose:

To help you honor your loved one's memory in ways that bring comfort instead of pain and to learn how to carry their presence forward as part of your healing journey.

Step 1: Memory Mapping

Take a sheet of paper and write your loved one's name in the center. Around their name, draw lines to create a "memory map."

In each bubble, jot down a memory, phrase, smell, sound, or habit that reminds you of them. Don't censor it, just write freely.

Next, circle three memories that bring warmth rather than deep pain. Reflect on what those specific memories teach you about love, resilience, or life.

Ask yourself: What can I carry forward from these memories into my daily life?

Step 2: The Legacy Journal

Write a short letter to your loved one that starts with:

"You may not be here, but your love still guides me when…"

Finish that sentence in as many ways as you can.

Then, write how you've changed since their passing — not only what you've lost, but what you've learned.

This can be revisited once a month as part of your ongoing healing ritual. Over time, it becomes a living document of growth and remembrance.

Step 3: Acts of Living Tribute

Think of one way to embody something they valued — volunteering, mentoring, creating, laughing more, traveling, or simply showing kindness.

Make a plan to do it this week.

Example: If they loved nature, take a walk in their favorite park and pick up litter in their honor.

Afterward, write a few sentences about how it made you feel. Notice how grief transforms when expressed through action.

Reflection Prompt:

Write a paragraph titled "Their Love Still Lives Through Me."

Describe how your loved one continues to shape who you are, what you believe, and how you love.

Let it remind you that grief isn't about holding on to pain — it's about holding on to meaning.

References

Boelen, P. A., van den Hout, M. A., & van den Bout, J. (2006). A cognitive-behavioral conceptualization of complicated grief. Clinical Psychology: Science and Practice, 13(2), 109–128.

Kabat-Zinn, J. (2003). Mindfulness-based interventions in context: Past, present, and future. Clinical Psychology: Science and Practice, 10(2), 144–156.

Klass, D., Silverman, P. R., & Nickman, S. L. (Eds.). (1996). Continuing bonds: New understandings of grief. Taylor & Francis.

Neimeyer, R. A. (2012). Techniques of grief therapy: Creative practices for counseling the bereaved. Routledge.

Pennebaker, J. W., & Seagal, J. D. (1999). Forming a story: The health benefits of narrative. Journal of Clinical Psychology, 55(10), 1243–1254

Romanoff, B. D., & Terenzio, M. (1998). Rituals and the grieving process. Death Studies, 22(8), 697–711.

Chapter 12

Signs and Synchronicities

The Comfort of Feeling Their Presence

In the midst of grief, many people report experiencing signs, synchronicities, or moments that feel like connections to their loved ones. These experiences can provide profound comfort, offering a sense of presence and continuity even after death. We explore the phenomenon of signs and synchronicities, the role of dreams and visitations in processing grief, and how to find meaning in the seemingly mundane.

The Language of the Universe

How to Recognize Signs from Your Loved One

Signs from a loved one can take many forms a sudden breeze, a song on the radio, or a fleeting scent. These moments often feel deeply personal and meaningful, as though your loved one is reaching out to you from beyond.

The Psychology of Signs and Synchronicities

From a psychological perspective, signs and synchronicities can be understood as a form of symbolic communication. According to Jung (1960), synchronicities are meaningful coincidences that reflect the interconnectedness of the psyche and the external world. In the context of grief, these experiences can serve as a bridge between the physical and spiritual realms, providing comfort and reassurance.

Research suggests that many bereaved individuals find solace in interpreting signs as messages from their loved ones (Hsu, Kahn, & Zimmerman, 2008). These experiences can help alleviate feelings of isolation and reinforce the feeling that a connection still remains.

How to Recognize and Interpret Signs

Pay Attention to Patterns: Notice if certain symbols, animals, or events repeatedly appear in your life. These patterns may hold personal significance and could be interpreted as signs from your loved one.

Trust Your Intuition: If something feels meaningful or significant, trust your intuition. Grief can heighten your sensitivity to subtle cues, allowing you to perceive connections that others might overlook.

Keep a Journal: Document your experiences of signs and synchronicities in a journal. Over time, you may begin to notice themes or patterns that provide deeper insight into their meaning.

Dreams and Visitations

The Role of Dreams in Processing Grief

Dreams are a powerful medium through which the subconscious mind processes emotions and experiences. For many people, dreams of a loved one can feel vivid and real, leaving them with a feeling of closeness and reassurance.

The Science of Grief Dreams

Grief dreams are a common phenomenon, with studies suggesting that up to 60% of bereaved individuals experience them (Barrett, 2001). These dreams can take various forms, from comforting visitations to distressing nightmares. While some dreams may reflect unresolved emotions, others can provide a sense of closure or reassurance.

Visitation dreams, in particular, are often described as profoundly meaningful. In these dreams, the deceased appears to convey a message of love, forgiveness, or guidance. Such experiences can help the bereaved feel a continued bond with their loved one (Hsu et al., 2008, Klass, Silverman, & Nickman, 1996).

How to Engage with Grief Dreams

Reflect on the Dream's Message: After a grief dream, take time to reflect on its content and emotional tone. Consider what the dream might be trying to communicate or resolve.

Share the Dream with Others: Sharing your dream with a trusted friend, family member, or therapist can help you process its meaning and significance.

Use Dreams as a Source of Comfort: If a dream brings you comfort, revisit it in your mind or write about it in a journal. This can help reinforce the sense of connection and reassurance it provides.

When Coincidences Feel Like Connections

Finding Meaning in the Mundane

In the aftermath of loss, even the most ordinary events can take on profound significance. A chance encounter, a meaningful song, or a random object can feel like a message from your loved one. These moments, often dismissed as coincidence, can become powerful sources of comfort and meaning.

The Role of Meaning-Making in Grief

Finding meaning during grief can be an important part of healing. As Neimeyer (2001) explains, meaning-making involves rebuilding a feeling of coherence and purpose after a profound loss. In this process, people often become more aware of moments that feel symbolic or significant. Coincidences and synchronicities can take on personal meaning, helping the bereaved feel that their relationship with the person who died still holds significance. Experiences like these are often understood as part of what grief scholars describe as continuing bonds, the ongoing psychological connection people maintain with loved ones after death (Klass, Silverman, & Nickman, 1996).

For example, someone might notice a feather on the ground and think of a loved one who had a special connection to birds.

Moments like this can bring quiet comfort, reminding us that memories and love do not simply disappear.

How to Embrace Synchronicities

After a loss, many people notice small moments that feel unexpectedly meaningful. Whether we call them coincidences, reminders, or simple moments of reflection, these experiences can become part of how we carry our memories forward.

Remain attentive to everyday moments.

Grief can heighten our awareness of the world around us. A familiar song, a feather on the ground, or a place that suddenly brings back a memory may feel significant. Rather than dismissing these moments, allow yourself to pause and reflect on what they evoke. Often, it is simply the memory of the person and the love you shared that rise to the surface.

Create personal ways to honor those moments.

Some people choose to mark these experiences in small ways. If an object or event reminds you of your loved one, you might keep it, write about it, or quietly acknowledge it. For example, someone who often finds pennies that remind them of a loved one may begin saving them or carrying one as a quiet reminder of that person.

Talk about these experiences with others who understand.

Sharing these memories or meaningful memories with trusted friends, family members, or support groups can be comforting. When people speak openly about these moments, it often deepens the feeling that the relationship and the love behind it are still part of their lives.

Exercise: The Signs Journal

Purpose: To help you recognize, interpret, and find comfort in the small moments that feel like messages from your loved one.

Instructions:

1. Create a dedicated notebook or use a section of your journal labeled "Signs and Synchronicities."

2. Over the next two weeks, jot down any moments that stand out, such as a song playing at the right time, a familiar scent, a dream, or an unexpected coincidence.

3. Write the date, what happened, and how it made you feel in that moment.

4. At the end of the two weeks, review your notes. Notice any patterns, symbols, or recurring themes.

5. Reflect: Do these experiences bring comfort, connection, or guidance?

Reflection Prompt:

"If love is energy, where have I felt its presence lately?"

Exercise 2: The Dream Reflection

Purpose: To process emotional healing through dreams and subconscious imagery.

Instructions:

1. Keep a small notebook beside your bed.

2. When you wake from a dream involving your loved one, write down as much detail as you remember — even fragments.

3. Don't analyze right away. After a week or two, read your notes and circle any feelings that stand out — peace, guilt, comfort, confusion.

4. In your journal, write a short reflection on what message or emotion your subconscious might be helping you process.

Reflection Prompt:

"What might my dreams be trying to help me understand or release?"

Exercise 3: Meaning in the Mundane

Purpose: To cultivate awareness of symbolic connections that bring peace.

Instructions:

1. Choose one ordinary daily activity — walking, making coffee, driving — and commit to doing it mindfully.

2. During that time, open your awareness. Notice sights, sounds, or feelings that seem significant.

3. Afterward, write down one small thing that stood out and what it reminded you of.

4. Consider whether these moments feel like gentle reminders that you're not alone.

Reflection Prompt:

"What everyday moments remind me that love still surrounds me, even in small ways?"

References

Barrett, D. (2001). *The committee of sleep: How artists, scientists, and athletes use dreams for creative problem-solving—and how you can too.* Crown.

Hsu, M., Kahn, J., & Zimmerman, M. (2008). Spiritual experiences of the bereaved: Meaning-making after loss. *Journal of Humanistic Psychology*, 48(2), 198–222.

Jung, C. G. (1960). *Synchronicity: An acausal connecting principle.* Princeton University Press.

Klass, D., Silverman, P. R., & Nickman, S. L. (1996). *Continuing bonds: New understandings of grief.* Taylor & Francis.

Neimeyer, R. A. (2001). *Meaning reconstruction and the experience of loss.* American Psychological Association.

Chapter 13

The Power of Rituals

How Traditions, Faith, and Personal Rituals Help with Healing

Rituals have been a cornerstone of human culture for millennia, serving as a bridge between the past and the present, the tangible and the intangible. In the context of grief, rituals can provide structure, meaning, and a sense of continuity in the face of loss. This chapter explores the transformative power of rituals, from creating new traditions that honor your loved one to finding solace in faith and spirituality. We will also examine how daily rituals can serve as small but powerful acts of healing.

Creating New Traditions

Honoring Your Loved One in Unique Ways

When a loved one dies, the traditions you once shared may feel incomplete or painful. Yet, creating new traditions can be a powerful way to honor their memory while forging a path forward. These new rituals can serve as a testament to the enduring bond you share with your loved one, even in their absence.

The Role of Rituals in Grief

Rituals can bring structure to a time that often feels chaotic. Romanoff and Terenzio (1998) note that rituals allow people to express grief outwardly, giving form to emotions that may otherwise feel overwhelming. By creating space for remembrance and reflection, rituals can help the bereaved acknowledge both the loss and the continuing significance of the relationship.

New traditions can take many forms. What matters most is that they feel authentic and meaningful to those involved.

Examples of New Traditions

Annual Remembrance Gatherings

Some families choose to gather once a year to remember their loved one. This might take place on a birthday, anniversary, or another meaningful date. Sharing stories, lighting candles, or preparing a favorite meal can keep memories alive while strengthening family connections.

Memory Boxes

A memory box filled with photographs, letters, or small keepsakes can become a place where memories are safely held.

Some people open the box on special occasions or when they feel the need to reconnect with those memories.

Creative Tributes

Creative expression can offer another path through grief. Planting a garden, creating artwork, writing a poem, or assembling a scrapbook can transform memories into lasting tributes.

Acts of Kindness

Many people honor their loved one by doing something kind in their name, volunteering, donating to a meaningful cause, or helping someone in need. These acts can extend the spirit of the person who died into the lives of others.

The Role of Faith and Spirituality

Finding Solace in Belief Systems

For many people, faith and spirituality provide a profound source of comfort and meaning in the face of loss. Whether through organized religion, personal spirituality, or a connection to nature, belief systems can offer a framework for understanding grief and finding hope.

The Intersection of Grief and Spirituality

Spirituality often plays a central role in the grieving process, providing a sense of connection to something greater than oneself. As Pargament (1997) notes, spirituality can help individuals find meaning in their suffering, fostering a sense of peace and acceptance. This is particularly true in the context of loss, where questions about life, death, and the afterlife often arise.

Faith communities can also provide a supportive network of individuals who share similar beliefs and values. This sense of belonging can be incredibly healing, offering both emotional and practical support during difficult times.

How to Incorporate Faith and Spirituality into Your Grief Journey

Engage in Spiritual Practices: Participate in practices that resonate with your beliefs, such as prayer, meditation, or attending religious services. These practices can provide a sense of grounding and connection.

Seek Guidance from Spiritual Leaders: Reach out to a spiritual leader or counselor for support and guidance. They can help you navigate the spiritual questions that often arise in grief.

Connect with Nature: For those who find spirituality in nature, spending time outdoors can be a powerful way to feel connected to something greater. Consider creating a nature-based ritual, such as planting a tree or scattering ashes in a meaningful location.

Explore Spiritual Literature: Reading spiritual or religious texts can provide comfort and insight. Look for books, poems, or scriptures that address themes of loss, hope, and resilience.

Daily Rituals for Healing

Small Practices to Bring Comfort and Peace

While grand gestures and annual traditions are important, daily rituals can also play a crucial role in the healing process. These small, consistent practices can provide a sense of stability and comfort, helping you navigate the ups and downs of grief.

The Power of Daily Rituals

Daily rituals serve as anchors in the storm of grief, offering moments of calm and reflection. As Kabat-Zinn (2003) describes, mindfulness-based practices can help individuals stay present and grounded, reducing the intensity of grief-related emotions. These practices can be as simple as lighting a candle, writing in a journal, or taking a few moments to breathe deeply.

Examples of Daily Healing Rituals

Morning Reflection: Start your day with a few moments of reflection. This could involve reading an inspirational quote, setting an intention for the day, or simply sitting in silence.

Gratitude Practice: Each day, write down three things you are grateful for. This practice can help shift your focus from loss to the positive aspects of your life.

Evening Candle Lighting: Light a candle in honor of your loved one each evening. Use this time to reflect on your day and feel their presence.

Mindful Movement: Engage in a daily movement practice, such as yoga, walking, or stretching. Focus on the sensations in your body and the rhythm of your breath.

Journaling: Spend a few minutes each day writing about your thoughts and feelings. This can help you process your emotions and track your progress over time.

Exercise: Building Your Healing Ritual

1. Reflect on Past Traditions

Think about the rituals, holidays, or faith-based practices that once brought comfort or connection. Which ones still hold meaning for you now, and which feel too painful or hollow?

Write a short reflection on what you miss most about these traditions.

Note one aspect you could reintroduce or reshape to honor your loved one in a gentler way.

2. Create a Personal Ritual

Design one small, repeatable act that helps you stay connected while also moving forward. It can be as simple as:

Lighting a candle every Sunday night.

Visiting a favorite spot on their birthday.

Cooking their favorite meal once a month and sharing stories about them.

Listening to a song that reminds you of them and journaling afterward.

3. Faith or Spiritual Expression

If faith or spirituality is part of your life, write or speak a short prayer, affirmation, or meditation that centers on peace and gratitude rather than loss.

Example: "I carry your love with me in every step forward."

Say or write it at the same time each day for a week.

4. Passing the Light

Invite one trusted person to join you in your ritual—perhaps to light a candle together, share a memory, or do something meaningful in your loved one's honor.

Notice how including others shifts the feeling of grief into shared remembrance.

References

Kabat-Zinn, J. (2003). Mindfulness-based interventions in context: Past, present, and future. Clinical Psychology: Science and Practice, 10(2), 144–156. https://doi.org/10.1093/clipsy.bpg016

Klass, D., Silverman, P. R., & Nickman, S. L. (1996). *Continuing bonds: New understandings of grief.* Taylor & Francis.

Neimeyer, R. A. (2001). *Meaning reconstruction and the experience of loss.* American Psychological Association.

Pargament, K. I. (1997). The psychology of religion and coping: Theory, research, practice. Guilford Press.

Romanoff, B. D., & Terenzio, M. (1998). Rituals and the grieving process. Death Studies, 22(8),

Stroebe, M., Schut, H., & Stroebe, W. (2007). Health outcomes of bereavement. *The Lancet, 370*(9603), 1960–1973. https://doi.org/10.1016/S0140-6736(07)61816-9

Chapter 14

Lessons from Loss

Finding Wisdom and Purpose in Pain

Grief is often described as a journey, one that transforms us in profound and unexpected ways. While the pain of loss can feel overwhelming, it can also be a catalyst for growth, wisdom, and resilience. In time, some people discover that loss also deepens their understanding of compassion, resilience, and the fragile beauty of life that can emerge from grief, from gaining a new perspective on life, to discovering strength you never knew you had.

The Gift of Perspective

How Loss Changes Your Outlook on Life

One of the most significant ways grief reshapes life is through perspective. Loss has a way of stripping away the trivial and revealing what truly matters. This newfound clarity can lead to a deeper appreciation for life and a renewed sense of purpose.

The Transformative Power of Grief

Grief often forces us to confront the fragility of life, leading us to reevaluate our priorities. Neimeyer (2001) observes that meaning-making in grief involves reconstructing our understanding of the world and our place in it. This process can lead to a deeper appreciation of relationships, experiences, and the present moment.

For example, many people find that after a loss, they become more intentional about how they spend their time and energy. They may prioritize relationships, pursue long-held dreams, or adopt a more mindful approach to life.

How to Embrace the Gift of Perspective

Reflect on Your Values: Take time to reflect on what matters most to you. Consider how your loss has influenced your priorities and how you can align your life with your values.

Practice Mindfulness: Cultivate a mindful approach to life, focusing on the present moment and savoring the small joys. This can help you stay grounded and appreciative.

Set Intentional Goals: Use your newfound perspective to set goals that align with your values and aspirations. Whether it's strengthening relationships, pursuing a passion, or giving back to others, let your grief guide you toward meaningful action.

Turning Pain into Purpose

Using Grief as a Catalyst for Growth

While grief is inherently painful, it can also be a powerful catalyst for personal growth and transformation. Some people find that their loss inspires them to make positive changes in their lives, from pursuing new passions to helping others who are grieving.

The Concept of Post-Traumatic Growth

Post-traumatic growth refers to the positive psychological changes that can occur as a result of struggling with highly challenging life circumstances (Tedeschi & Calhoun, 2004). In the context of grief, this might involve developing greater empathy, finding new meaning in life, or discovering untapped strengths.

For example, some individuals channel their grief into advocacy work, raising awareness about issues related to their loss. Others may find healing in creative expression, using art, writing, or music to process their emotions and inspire others.

How to Turn Pain into Purpose

Identify Your Strengths: Reflect on the strengths and qualities that have emerged from your grief. How can you use these strengths to make a positive impact?

Pursue Meaningful Activities: Engage in activities that bring you a sense of purpose and fulfillment. This could involve volunteering, mentoring, or pursuing a creative project.

Share Your Story: Consider sharing your grief journey with others, whether through writing, speaking, or participating in support groups. Sharing your story may offer comfort or encouragement to others who are grieving.

The Strength You Never Knew You Had

Discovering Resilience in Adversity

Grief often reveals a depth of strength and resilience that may not have been visible before. While the journey through loss is undeniably difficult, it can also be a testament to the human capacity for endurance and growth.

The Nature of Resilience

Resilience is the ability to adapt and thrive in the face of adversity. It is not about avoiding pain or hardship but about finding ways to navigate and grow through it (Bonanno, 2004). In the context of grief, resilience involves finding meaning, maintaining hope, and cultivating a sense of agency.

For some, the grieving process reveals an inner strength that may not have been recognized before. This strength can manifest as the ability to face difficult emotions, the courage to rebuild a life after loss, or the determination to honor a loved one's memory.

How to Cultivate Resilience

Acknowledge Your Strength: Take time to recognize and celebrate the strength you have shown in the face of loss. Reflect on the challenges you have overcome and the progress you have made.

Build a Support Network: Surround yourself with people who uplift and support you. A strong support network can provide encouragement and help you navigate difficult times.

Practice Self-Compassion: Be kind and patient with yourself as you navigate grief. Recognize that healing is a gradual process and that it's okay to have difficult days.

Focus on Growth: Embrace the lessons and opportunities for growth that emerge from your grief. Let your loss inspire you to live a more meaningful and purposeful life.

Exercise: Building Your Healing Ritual

1. **Reflect on Past Traditions**

Think about the rituals, holidays, or faith-based practices that once brought comfort or connection. Which ones still hold meaning for you now, and which feel too painful or hollow?

Write a short reflection on what you miss most about these traditions.

Note one aspect you could reintroduce or reshape to honor your loved one in a gentler way.

2. Create a Personal Ritual

Design one small, repeatable act that helps you stay connected while also moving forward. It can be as simple as:

Lighting a candle every Sunday night.

Visiting a favorite spot on their birthday.

Cooking their favorite meal once a month and sharing stories about them.

Listening to a song that reminds you of them and journaling afterward.

3. Faith or Spiritual Expression

If faith or spirituality is part of your life, write or speak a short prayer, affirmation, or meditation that centers on peace and gratitude rather than loss.

Example: “I carry your love with me in every step forward.”

Say or write it at the same time each day for a week.

4. Passing the Light

Invite one trusted person to join you in your ritual, perhaps to light a candle together, share a memory, or do something meaningful in your loved one's honor.

Notice how including others shifts the feeling of grief into shared remembrance.

References

Bonanno, G. A. (2004). Loss, trauma, and human resilience: Have we underestimated the human capacity to thrive after extremely aversive events? *American Psychologist, 59*(1), 20–28. https://doi.org/10.1037/0003-066X.59.1.20

Neimeyer, R. A. (2001). Meaning reconstruction and the experience of loss. American Psychological Association.

Tedeschi, R. G., & Calhoun, L. G. (2004). Posttraumatic growth: Conceptual foundations and empirical evidence. *Psychological Inquiry, 15*(1), 1–18. https://doi.org/10.1207/s15327965pli1501_01

Chapter 15

The Art of Letting Go Without Forgetting

Balancing Remembrance and Acceptance

Letting go after loss does not mean abandoning the memory of the person we love. It means learning how to release the pain that binds us to the moment of loss while preserving the memories that give life meaning. Over time, forgiveness, acceptance, and remembrance can transform grief into a lasting connection, one that allows love to remain present as life continues.

The Gentle Art of Release

Grief reshapes the way we love. In the beginning, the idea of "letting go" feels impossible, like betrayal. The heart resists it. You may think, If I stop holding on so tightly, will that mean I've forgotten them? The truth is, letting go has never been about forgetting; it is about making peace with what remains. It is about allowing love to take on a new form grounded in gratitude rather than chained to sorrow.

In many experiences of grief, there comes a turning point when the sharpness of pain begins to soften. That moment doesn't erase the ache, but it changes its rhythm. Memories still come, but they no longer cut as deeply. They arrive more like gentle waves than storms. Over time, some people discover that holding on to suffering does not preserve the relationship; instead, it can keep them caught in cycles of longing. Releasing that grip can create space for memory to breathe and for love to evolve (Neimeyer, 2001).

Imagine your heart as a room once filled with the noise of grief. In the beginning, every object inside carries the vibration of loss. But as time passes, the room changes. You begin to rearrange things. You keep what matters: photos, laughter, lessons, and release what keeps you from walking freely through that space. That is the art of letting go without forgetting: learning to live in the same room with your memories but no longer letting them block the light.

Acceptance doesn't come in one grand revelation. It happens in moments, small decisions to live again. Choosing to smile without guilt. To visit their favorite place without breaking down. To let yourself dream about a future that doesn't include them physically but still honors their presence. That is how remembrance and release learn to coexist.

What It Means to Let Go

Releasing Pain, Not Memories

Letting go is not an act of abandonment; it's an act of love. It means freeing yourself from the emotional chains that keep you reliving the moment of loss instead of remembering the fullness of life that came before it. Some people confuse letting go with forgetting, but the two couldn't be more different. Forgetting erases; letting go transforms.

You do not let go of the person. You let go of the pain that clouds their memory. When you stop replaying the "what ifs" and "if onlys," you make room for the moments that once brought joy. You begin to see the story of your loved one as more than their final chapter. You start remembering their laughter, their quirks, their lessons, and the ways they shaped who you are.

Letting go also means accepting that you cannot change what has already happened. It's a gentle surrender, not a loss of control. You stop fighting time. You allow your heart to catch its breath. This is how peace begins to grow in a quiet, almost imperceptible way. One morning, you wake up and realize the pain hasn't disappeared, but it no longer owns you.

Letting go is the decision to live fully while still carrying the memory. It's a way of saying: You will always be part of me, but I must learn to walk forward. In grief research, this shift is often described as maintaining a continuing bond with the person who died while adapting to life in their physical absence (Klass, Silverman, & Nickman, 1996).

The Role of Forgiveness

Letting Go of Guilt, Regret, and Anger

Forgiveness can act as the bridge between remembrance and emotional freedom. After a loss, people often carry invisible burdens such as guilt for things left unsaid, anger at how events unfolded, or regret about what might have been done differently. These feelings are a natural part of grief, but when they remain unresolved, they can slow the healing process.

Forgiving yourself is often the hardest part. Thoughts such as "I should have seen the signs" or "I wish I had been there more" can repeat in painful loops. Yet grief researchers note that self-blame frequently emerges during bereavement as the mind tries to regain a sense of control over an uncontrollable event (Neimeyer, 2001). Self-forgiveness begins with recognizing that decisions were made with the knowledge and capacity available at the time.

Forgiving others, whether a doctor, a family member, or even the person who passed, can also be part of the process. It doesn't mean excusing harm or pretending everything is fine. It means refusing to let resentment control your heart. When anger lives at the center of grief, peace cannot enter. When you forgive, you reclaim your energy and redirect it toward love.

Sometimes, forgiveness takes the form of simple acknowledgement: I release what I cannot change. Each time you speak that truth, you untangle another knot. In time, forgiveness softens the landscape of grief. It doesn't erase the scars—it simply allows light to shine through them.

Creating a New Relationship with the Past:

Honoring Without Clinging

As the intensity of grief begins to ease, a new question often emerges: "Who am I now, in relation to what I've lost?" The past doesn't disappear; it becomes a part of your foundation on which the future is built. Healing asks you to build a new relationship with someone based on honoring rather than clinging.

To honor the past is to recognize its value without letting it define the present. Some people find comfort in revisiting places, keeping photos, or celebrating anniversaries, but from a space of gratitude rather than sorrow. The goal is not to stop missing them; it's to integrate their memory into your ongoing life story.

Rituals often play an important role in this transition. Lighting a candle on a birthday, creating a memory box, or sharing stories about a loved one can transform grief into legacy. Such rituals help maintain a continuing bond with the deceased while allowing life to move forward (Romanoff & Terenzio, 1998).

Creating a new relationship with the past also means allowing yourself to grow beyond it. You can love someone deeply and still move toward new experiences, friendships, and possibilities. The past becomes a companion rather than a cage. When you honor your memories this way, you give them the dignity they deserve they become light you carry, not chains you drag.

Reflection: The Weight You Choose to Carry

There is quiet strength in those who learn to live with both love and loss. They understand that grief does not completely disappear; it simply changes form. The ache becomes softer, the memories clearer, the love purer. Letting go doesn't mean you've lost what mattered; it means you've made space for life to continue. You've learned to carry your person differently—inside, where no distance or time can touch them.

Over time, the past may begin to whisper instead of shout. You start to see signs of healing in small things, your ability to laugh again, to plan ahead, to breathe without the heaviness in your chest. You realize the goal was never to "get over" them, but to bring them with you in a way that allows you to live freely. The art of letting go is learning that remembrance and acceptance can exist in the same breath.

Conclusion: Love That Outlives Loss

Letting go without forgetting is not a single act but a lifelong practice. You will revisit your memories many times, and each time, they will mean something slightly different. Some days, they will make you cry. Other days, they will make you smile. Both are expressions of love.

The beauty of this process lies in balance. You are not replacing or diminishing the person you lost; you are redefining the space they hold within you. You are learning to honor them by living a life worthy of their memory.

So when people tell you to move on, remember you don't have to move on; you can move forward. And every step you take, no matter how small, carries the quiet strength of someone who has learned to let go of pain while holding onto love.

Exercise: The Art of Letting Go Without Forgetting

Purpose:

This exercise helps you explore what it truly means to let go—releasing pain without erasing memory. It guides you toward forgiveness, emotional peace, and a new relationship with your past.

Step 1: Releasing Pain, Not Memories

Think of someone, an event, or a period in your life that still brings a wave of pain when remembered. You don't need to write their name—just the feeling that arises.

Prompt:

1. What memory or moment still feels heavy for you?

2. What emotion do you associate most with this memory—anger, sadness, guilt, regret, or something else?

3. If the pain could speak, what would it say it still needs? (Closure, apology, understanding, acknowledgment, etc.)

Reflection:

Letting go doesn't mean forgetting what happened—it means freeing yourself from reliving it daily.

Step 2: The Role of Forgiveness

Forgiveness is not about excusing what happened—it's about releasing your attachment to the anger that keeps you tied to it.

Prompt:

1. Who or what are you ready to forgive, even if they never say "I'm sorry"?

2. What part of yourself needs forgiveness—for choices made in pain, confusion, or fear?

3. Imagine forgiveness as a bridge between your past and your peace. What does stepping onto that bridge feel like?

Reflection:

Sometimes forgiveness is less about others and more about reclaiming your own energy.

Step 3: Creating a New Relationship with the Past

You can honor your past without living in it. This step helps you redefine what remembering means.

Prompt:

1. What lesson or strength did that experience leave you with?

2. How can you honor the memory in a healthy way (through journaling, art, service, or gratitude)?

3. Write one sentence that reclaims your story:

Example: "This memory no longer defines my pain—it defines my growth."

Step 4: Letting Go Ritual

Find a quiet space. Write a word or sentence that represents what you're ready to release—anger, guilt, regret, shame.

Fold the paper, take a deep breath, and either:

Burn it safely (symbolic cleansing),

Tear it into pieces and throw it away, or

Bury it under soil to symbolize transformation.

As you do, say quietly:

"I honor what I've lived through, but I no longer live in it."

Step 5: Acceptance Journal

Spend five minutes writing freely, without stopping, on this prompt:

"What does peace look like for me when I stop holding on?"

Then circle one word that captures how you want to move forward—peace, balance, freedom, clarity, or grace—and write it at the top of a new page. That word becomes your anchor for this next season of healing.

Final Reflection

Letting go is not forgetting. It's remembering with gratitude instead of grief, love instead of loss, and meaning instead of pain.

"You cannot change what was, but you can change what it means to you."

References

Klass, D., Silverman, P. R., & Nickman, S. L. (1996). *Continuing bonds: New understandings of grief.* Taylor & Francis.

Neimeyer, R. A. (2001). *Meaning reconstruction and the experience of loss.* American Psychological Association.

Romanoff, B. D., & Terenzio, M. (1998). Rituals and the grieving process. *Death Studies, 22*(8), 697–711.

Chapter 16

Grieving in Public vs. Private

Balancing Personal Grief with Societal Expectations

Grief is a deeply personal experience, yet it is often shaped by the expectations of the world around us. The tension between public and private mourning can add another layer of complexity to an already difficult journey. Many people feel pressure to express grief in ways others understand, even when those expressions do not reflect their true experience. Creating boundaries and allowing space for private reflection can help protect the personal nature of grief and honor the uniqueness of each person's journey

The Pressure to "Perform" Grief

How Society Shapes Our Mourning

From the moment we experience loss, societal expectations begin to influence how we grieve. These expectations can manifest in subtle and overt ways, from assumptions about how long mourning should last to beliefs about how emotions should be expressed. When those expectations clash with personal experience, the grieving process can become even more difficult.

Societal Norms and Grief

Societal norms around grief are often shaped by cultural, religious, and historical contexts. For example, in many Western cultures, there is an expectation that grief should be time-limited and that individuals should "move on" after a certain period (Stroebe, Hansson, Schut, & Stroebe, 2008). This can lead to feelings of inadequacy or shame for those who continue to grieve beyond the socially accepted timeframe.

Additionally, public expressions of grief are often scrutinized. Those who grieve openly may be labeled as "dramatic," while those who grieve privately may be seen as "cold" or "unfeeling." This dichotomy can create a sense of isolation and confusion for the bereaved.

The Impact of Social Media

The growth of social media has added another dimension to public mourning. Platforms such as Facebook and Instagram have become places where people share tributes, memories, and expressions of grief. For some, these spaces provide support and connection; for others, they can create pressure to present grief in a particular way (Walter, 2015).

Posting a tribute or memorial message may bring comforting responses, but it can also invite unwanted commentary or comparisons with how others grieve. Navigating these public spaces often requires balancing the desire for support with the need to protect one's emotional well-being.

Strategies for Navigating Societal Expectations

Acknowledge Your Feelings: Recognize that your grief is valid, regardless of societal expectations. Allow yourself to feel and express your emotions in ways that feel authentic to you.

Challenge Unrealistic Norms: Question the societal norms that dictate how and when you should grieve. Remember that grief rarely evolves in neat stages and that there is no "right" way to mourn.

Seek Supportive Communities: Surround yourself with individuals who respect and validate your grief journey. This might include friends, family, or support groups where you can share your experiences without judgment.

Creating Boundaries

Protecting Your Grief Journey from External Judgment

In a world that often feels intrusive, creating boundaries is essential for protecting your grief journey. Boundaries allow you to honor your emotions and needs while shielding yourself from external pressures and judgments.

The Importance of Boundaries in Grief

Boundaries serve as a protective barrier, helping you navigate the complexities of grief without being overwhelmed by external influences. According to Neimeyer (2012), setting boundaries can help you maintain a sense of agency and control in a situation that often feels chaotic and unpredictable.

For example, you may choose to limit your interactions with individuals who are dismissive of your grief or who offer unsolicited advice. Similarly, you might set boundaries around how and when you engage with social media, ensuring that it serves as a source of support rather than stress.

How to Establish and Maintain Boundaries

Communicate Your Needs: Clearly communicate your needs and boundaries to those around you. For example, you might let friends and family know that you need space or that you prefer not to discuss certain topics.

Practice Self-Advocacy: Advocate for yourself by asserting your boundaries in a respectful but firm manner. Remember that it is okay to say no to requests or invitations that feel overwhelming.

Create Physical and Emotional Space: Designate a physical space where you can retreat and process your emotions without interruption. This might be a quiet room in your home or a favorite outdoor spot.

Limit Exposure to Triggers: Identify and limit your exposure to situations or individuals that exacerbate your grief. This might involve unfollowing certain social media accounts or avoiding events that feel emotionally taxing.

The Power of Privacy

Some Grief Is Meant to Be Personal

While public expressions of grief can be healing for some, others find solace in privacy. For many, grief is a deeply personal experience that feels too intimate to share with the world. Honoring this need for privacy can be an essential part of the healing process.

The Role of Privacy in Grief

Privacy allows individuals to process their emotions without the pressure of external expectations or judgments. Continuing bonds theory suggests that maintaining an internal relationship with the deceased often occurs through personal reflection and private remembrance (Klass, Silverman, & Nickman, 1996).

For some, privacy is a way to protect the sacredness of their relationship with the deceased. Sharing their grief publicly may feel like a violation of that intimacy, making private mourning a more authentic and meaningful choice.

How to Honor Your Need for Privacy

Create Personal Rituals: Develop private rituals that allow you to honor your loved one in a way that feels meaningful to you. This might involve writing in a journal, lighting a candle, or spending time in nature.

Limit Public Expressions: If public expressions of grief feel uncomfortable, limit your engagement with social media or public memorials. Instead, focus on private acts of remembrance that align with your needs.

Seek One-on-One Support: If you prefer privacy, seek support from a trusted friend, family member, or therapist. These one-on-one interactions can provide a sense of connection without the pressure of public exposure.

Respect Your Timeline: Allow yourself to grieve at your own pace, without feeling pressured to share your journey with others. Remember that your grief is yours alone, and you have the right to process it in a way that feels authentic to you.

Exercise: The Strength in Surrender

Purpose:

This exercise helps you practice the art of surrender—not as weakness, but as wisdom. It teaches you how to release control, accept what you cannot change, and find peace in the present moment.

Step 1: Identifying What You're Holding On To

Before you can surrender, you must see what you're still gripping tightly.

Prompt:

1. What situation or person have you been trying to control or fix?

____

____

2. What do you fear might happen if you let go of control?

____

____

3. How does holding on make you feel? Physically or emotionally drained, anxious, tense, exhausted?

____

____

Reflection:

Control often gives us the illusion of safety, but surrender gives us real peace.

Step 2: The Circle of Control Exercise

Draw two circles—one inside the other. Label the inner circle "What I Can Control" and the outer circle "What I Cannot Control."

Examples to guide you:

Inner Circle (Control): Your reactions, effort, boundaries, kindness, mindset.

Outer Circle (No Control): Other people's choices, timing, outcomes, the past.

Prompt:

Write in each circle what applies to your current situation. Then take one deep breath and focus only on the inner circle.

Reflection:

Peace grows where control ends.

Step 3: The Power of Allowing

Allowing doesn't mean agreeing—it means recognizing reality without fighting it.

Prompt:

1. What truth have you been resisting?

2. What would it look like to simply allow things to be as they are for one day?

3. How might acceptance open a door that control has kept closed?

"When I stopped trying to force life, I discovered it was already unfolding for me."

Step 4: Breathing Practice for Release

Find a quiet space. Sit comfortably and close your eyes.

Inhale for 4 seconds, thinking "I welcome peace."

Hold for 4 seconds, thinking "I trust the process."

Exhale for 6 seconds, thinking "I release what I can't control."

Repeat this 5 times.

Afterward, write what came up for you:

Step 5: Reframing the Narrative

When we surrender, we often discover that letting go doesn't mean loss—it means making room for something better.

Prompt:

1. Finish this sentence: "By letting go of _______________, I create space for _______________."

2. Write one way surrender has already blessed your life in the past.

3. What would trusting life—just a little more—look like this week?

Step 6: The Surrender Statement

Write a short statement that captures what you are choosing to release and what you are choosing to trust.

Example:

"I release the need to control what isn't mine to carry.

I trust that peace will meet me where surrender begins."

Now, write your own:

Reflection:

____

____

Let this become a daily reminder. Read it whenever you feel yourself slipping back into control or fear.

Step 7: Gratitude After Surrender

Even in surrender, gratitude is grounding.

List three things that remain steady and good in your life, even when everything else feels uncertain.

1.____

2. ____

3. ____

"Surrender isn't giving up—it's giving over. You hand your fears to faith, and your need for control to peace."

Final Reflection

When we surrender, we stop wrestling with what is and start resting in what can be. The act of letting go is not passive—it's powerful.

It's saying, "I trust that life knows what it's doing, even when I don't."

References

Klass, D., Silverman, P. R., & Nickman, S. L. (Eds.). (1996). Continuing bonds: New understandings of grief. Taylor & Francis.

Neimeyer, R. A. (2012). Techniques of grief therapy: Creative practices for counseling the bereaved. Routledge.

Stroebe, M., Hansson, R. O., Schut, H., & Stroebe, W. (Eds.). (2008). Handbook ofereavement research and practice: Advances in theory and intervention. American Psychological Association.

Walter, T. (2015). New mourners, old mourners: Online memorial culture as a chapter in the history of mourning. *New Review of Hypermedia and Multimedia, 21*(1–2), 10–24.

Chapter 17

The Intersection of Grief and Identity

How Culture, Gender, and Age Shape the Grieving Process

Grief does not occur in isolation. Culture, age, gender, and life experiences all shape how we mourn, how others respond to our pain, and the rituals we use to remember those we have lost. These influences can shape both our understanding of loss and the support we receive from those around us. Recognizing the role of identity in grief can deepen empathy, strengthen connection, and help us care for one another with greater understanding.

Cultural Rituals and Expectations

How Traditions Influence Grief

Culture provides the framework through which we make sense of death. It dictates the rituals we observe, the words we use, and even the timeline we are "allowed" to grieve. In many ways, culture is the lens that gives grief both meaning and order.

The Role of Culture in Grief

Cultural beliefs and traditions provide structure and comfort during loss, creating predictable rituals that help mourners navigate chaos. As Rosenblatt (2008) explains, culture gives the bereaved a "road map" for expressing sorrow and reintegrating into social life. It defines who participates in mourning, how long it should last, and what public displays of emotion are acceptable.

For example, in many African and Caribbean traditions, funerals are celebrations of life; vibrant gatherings filled with music, color, and food that honor the deceased's spirit. In contrast, Western norms often emphasize restraint, solemnity, and composure, reflecting values of individualism and privacy (Walter, 2015). Neither approach is right or wrong; each reflects its society's values and beliefs about death.

Cultural expectations can also shape who is "allowed" to grieve. Some traditions give priority to immediate family, while others recognize extended kin or even community members as rightful mourners. When an individual's grief falls outside these boundaries, such as a same-sex partner in an unsupportive community, it can lead to disenfranchised grief, where their loss is not publicly validated (Doka, 2002).

Navigating Cultural Expectations

1. Honor Your Cultural Heritage: Lean into the traditions that bring you comfort and meaning. Lighting candles, wearing specific colors, cooking symbolic foods, or observing a mourning period can offer connection and continuity.

2. Respect Differences: When others grieve in ways that differ from your own, approach with curiosity rather than judgment. Grief is an expression of love filtered through culture.

3. Create a Hybrid Approach: For those from multicultural families or interfaith relationships, consider blending traditions. You might combine a Christian memorial service with a Buddhist prayer ritual or pair a Western funeral with African libations to honor ancestors.

4. Acknowledge Cultural Tensions: If your personal beliefs conflict with traditional norms, it's okay to adapt. Healing requires authenticity, not conformity.

Culture reminds us that grief is both personal and collective. When embraced thoughtfully, it can be a bridge between past and present - a way of remembering who we are and where we come from.

Grief Across Generations

How Age Impacts the Way We Mourn

Grief does not look the same at every age. Our capacity to understand loss and express emotion evolves across the lifespan, influenced by developmental stage, cognitive ability, and life experience. Recognizing these differences allows families, caregivers, and communities to offer more age-appropriate support.

Grief in Childhood and Adolescence

Children's understanding of death depends on their developmental stage. According to Worden (2018), young children may view death as temporary or reversible, while adolescents begin to grasp its permanence but may struggle with the emotional complexity. Because children often lack the vocabulary to describe their pain, grief can surface through behavior like acting out, regression, or withdrawal (Silverman & Worden, 2012).

A child might reenact the funeral during play or ask repetitive questions about where their loved one "went." Teens, by contrast, may rebel or seek comfort from peers instead of adults. These reactions are not signs of maladjustment but expressions of confusion, fear, and yearning. Some young adults also find comfort in peer-based grief groups where they can talk with others navigating similar losses during the early stages of adulthood.

Adults can support grieving youth by maintaining routines, encouraging open communication, and providing creative outlets such as art, writing, or music. Above all, they need reassurance that their emotions, no matter how messy, are normal.

Grief in Adulthood

For adults, grief often competes with responsibility. Between work obligations, caregiving duties, and financial stress, adults may feel pressured to "hold it together." They might compartmentalize their pain or hide emotions to protect others. This internalization can delay healing or contribute to physical symptoms such as fatigue, insomnia, or anxiety (Stroebe et al., 2008).

Adult grief also varies depending on the relationship lost. Losing a spouse may bring identity confusion; losing a parent can evoke both childlike vulnerability and adult guilt; losing a child can shatter one's sense of purpose. Support at this stage should include practical help—meals, childcare, time off work—alongside emotional validation.

Grief in Older Adulthood

Later-life grief is often cumulative. Older adults may face multiple losses in a short span—friends, siblings, mobility, independence—and the weight of mortality grows heavier. As Neimeyer (2012) observes, older adults may grapple not only with bereavement but with existential questions about meaning and legacy.

Some older adults find solace in storytelling, passing on memories to younger generations. Others may struggle with isolation, especially when peers or partners have died. For them, grief support groups for seniors or volunteer opportunities can provide renewed connection and purpose.

Supporting Grieving Individuals Across Generations

1. Tailor Support to Developmental Needs: Adjust your approach based on age. Children benefit from play and routine; adolescents from autonomy and peer connection; adults from empathy and time; and elders from companionship and legacy-building.

2. Acknowledge Cumulative Grief: Recognize that multiple losses can compound emotional pain. Offer patience and consistent presence rather than rushed solutions.

3. Foster Intergenerational Connection: Encourage storytelling and shared remembrance between generations. A

grandparent's wisdom can comfort a grieving child just as a child's innocence can bring hope to an aging adult.

Grief, like life, is cyclical. Understanding its developmental variations helps us create a continuum of care that honors every stage of the human journey.

Gender and Grief - Societal Expectations for Men and Women in Mourning

Grief is universal, but the way we express it is often shaped by gender norms. Society teaches men and women—and increasingly, people of all gender identities—what emotions are "acceptable." These unspoken rules can either help or hinder healing.

Gendered Expressions of Grief

In many cultures, men are expected to remain stoic, suppress tears, and "be strong" for others. Women, conversely, are often encouraged to express vulnerability and nurture others' pain even when their own is unhealed (Doka & Martin, 2010).

These stereotypes can distort authentic grieving. A man who cries openly might be seen as weak; a woman who appears composed might be called cold. As a result, individuals can feel guilt or shame for not grieving "correctly."

Doka and Martin (2010) distinguish between intuitive grief, characterized by emotional expression, and instrumental grief, focused on cognitive or action-oriented coping (e.g., organizing a memorial). Neither style is superior; most people fall somewhere along the spectrum. The problem arises when social expectations devalue one form over the other.

The Impact of Expanding Gender Identities

Contemporary understandings of gender have made space for more fluid expressions of emotion. Nonbinary and transgender individuals, however, may face unique grief challenges—such as exclusion from family rituals or lack of acknowledgment for their relationships. Inclusive grief spaces that affirm diverse identities are critical for healing (Harper & O'Connor, 2022).

Breaking Free from Gendered Expectations

1. Challenge Stereotypes: Question the narratives that dictate how you "should" grieve. Strength and vulnerability are not opposites, they can coexist.

2. Seek Inclusive Support: Look for counselors or groups that affirm diverse gender identities and recognize varied emotional styles. Healing thrives in acceptance.

3. Encourage Open Dialogue: Talking about grief helps dismantle stigma. By sharing our experiences, we normalize emotional authenticity for everyone.

4. Model Emotional Balance: Parents and leaders can set examples by expressing grief in healthy, balanced ways—showing that emotion is not weakness but humanity.

By challenging outdated gender norms, we open pathways to more compassionate, holistic expressions of grief—for ourselves and others.

Intersectionality in Grief

When Culture, Gender, and Age Overlap

While each of these factors, culture, age, and gender, affects grief independently, their full impact emerges through intersectionality. The term, coined by Crenshaw (1989), refers to how overlapping aspects of identity shape one's experience of the world.

A young Latina woman may experience grief differently from an elderly Asian man or a middle-aged Black father. Cultural heritage, generational worldview, and gender norms intertwine to shape not only how grief is expressed but how it is received by society.

In some cultures, expressive mourning is encouraged; in others, restraint is expected. Older generations may conceal grief to maintain dignity, while younger individuals, raised in a digital environment, may express sorrow publicly online. Recognizing these intersections allows caregivers and communities to move beyond stereotypes and offer support that reflects each person's lived reality.

Creating Space for Individual Grief Identities

Grief counseling and community support must become culturally and socially informed. Therapists, clergy, and support group facilitators can cultivate inclusivity by asking open-ended questions such as, "What does mourning look like in your family?" or "How do your cultural or spiritual beliefs shape the way you honor your loved one?"

Listening with empathy and without assumptions allows people to feel seen and respected in their grief.

Finding Universality Within Diversity

What Connects Us All

Despite the vast differences in how people grieve, certain truths unite us. Across time, culture, and gender, grief reflects love. Whether expressed through tears, silence, song, or ritual, it stems from the same source: the human capacity for attachment.

Understanding the intersection of grief and identity does not erase these differences - it honors them. It allows us to see grief not as a fixed process but as a living, evolving experience shaped by who we are and where we come from.

Neimeyer (2012) reminds us that healing does not mean erasing grief but integrating it into a renewed sense of self. Recognizing the cultural, generational, and gendered dimensions of mourning can help transform loss into deeper empathy and appreciation for the resilience of the human spirit.

Exercise: Rewriting the Story - Turning Pain into Purpose

Purpose:

This exercise guides you through transforming painful experiences into personal strength and meaning. It helps you reclaim your narrative so that what once broke you now becomes what built you.

Step 1: Name the Story That Hurt You

Before you can rewrite your story, you must name it.

Think about the event, season, or loss that changed you. The goal isn't to relive it—it's to face it with new eyes.

Prompt:

1. What is the chapter of your life that still feels unfinished or heavy?

2. If that chapter had a title, what would it be?

(Example: "The Year Everything Fell Apart," "When I Lost Myself," "The Unanswered Goodbye")

3. What emotion do you still carry when you think of that story?

Reflection:

Pain loses power when it's named. Awareness is the first act of rewriting.

Step 2: Identifying the Turning Point

Every story shifts. Somewhere between hurt and healing, something in you began to change.

Prompt:

1. What moment, person, or realization helped you begin to see things differently?

2. What strength or quality did that experience awaken in you (resilience, empathy, courage, faith, patience)?

3. How are you different today because of what you survived?

"The same fire that burned you can become the light that guides you."

Step 3: Rewriting the Narrative

Now that you've identified growth, it's time to reframe the story from pain to purpose.

Exercise:

Complete these sentences slowly and honestly:

1. What I thought was the end of my story was actually the beginning of ______________________________.

2. This experience taught me that

____.

3. I no longer see myself as a victim of ______________, but as a survivor who ____________________________.

Reflection:

You cannot erase the past, but you can decide what it means going forward.

Step 4: From Wound to Wisdom

Sometimes pain becomes a teacher. What if what hurt you most also gave you something of value to offer others?

Prompt:

1. What lesson from your pain could help someone else right now?

2. Who might benefit from hearing what you've learned?

3. How could you share it—through conversation, art, mentoring, or writing?

Optional activity:

Write a short letter to your "younger self" or someone going through something similar. End with a message of hope.

Step 5: Reclaiming Your Power

Take back ownership of your story. Instead of asking "Why did this happen to me?" ask "What can I create because of it?"

Prompt:

1. What part of your story no longer defines you?

2. What new role are you writing for yourself now—healer, teacher, leader, advocate, survivor?

3. What would your story's new title be today?

(Example: "Becoming Whole," "The Strength I Never Knew," "Grace After the Storm")

"Your pain shaped you, but it doesn't own you. You are the author now."

Step 6: Purpose in Action

Transformation means taking your new awareness and putting it into motion.

Prompt:

1. What one small action can you take this week that aligns with your growth?

(Example: Reach out to help someone in need, forgive yourself, start journaling, volunteer, or simply rest.)

2. How will you remind yourself that you are living a new chapter?

3. Finish this affirmation:

"I am no longer defined by what broke me, but by what I built after."

Step 7: Reflection and Gratitude

Take a deep breath and reflect on where you are now compared to where you began.

Write three things you're grateful for that have come from your healing journey.

1.

____

____

2.

____

____

3.

____

____

Final Thought:

"The most powerful stories are not the ones we survive, they're the ones we transform."

References

Crenshaw, K. (1989). Demarginalizing the intersection of race and sex. *University of Chicago Legal Forum*, 1989(1), 139–167.

Doka, K. J. (2002). *Disenfranchised grief: New directions, challenges, and strategies for practice.* Research Press.

Doka, K. J., & Martin, T. L. (2010). *Grieving beyond gender: Understanding the ways men and women mourn.* Routledge.

Harper, A., & O'Connor, M. (2022). Identity-affirming approaches to grief counseling for LGBTQ+ individuals. *Death Studies*, 46(6), 1342–1352.

Neimeyer, R. A. (2012). *Techniques of grief therapy: Creative practices for counseling the bereaved.* Routledge.

Rosenblatt, P. C. (2008). *Grief across cultures: A review and research agenda.* In M. Stroebe et al. (Eds.), *Handbook of bereavement research and practice.* APA.

Silverman, P. R., & Worden, J. W. (2012). Children's reactions in the early months after the death of a parent. *American Journal of Orthopsychiatry*, 82(2), 145–156.

Stroebe, M., Hansson, R., Schut, H., & Stroebe, W. (2008). *Handbook of bereavement research and practice.* APA.

Walter, T. (2015). New mourners, old mourners: Online memorial culture as a chapter in the history of mourning. *New Review of Hypermedia and Multimedia*, 21(1-2), 10–24.

Worden, J. W. (2018). *Grief counseling and grief therapy* (5th ed.). Springer.

Part 4: Moving Forward with Love

Chapter 18

Rebuilding a Life Without Them

Redefining Yourself After Loss

Loss has a way of reshaping our lives in profound and unexpected ways. When someone we love dies, we are not only grieving their absence but also grappling with the loss of the life we once knew. Rebuilding a life without them becomes a journey of redefinition, rediscovery, and courage. This next section explores the process of navigating identity shifts after loss, finding meaning and joy again, and embracing the courage to begin a new chapter.

Who Am I Now?

Navigating Identity Shifts After Loss

The death of a loved one often forces us to confront fundamental questions about who we are and what our lives mean. Whether the deceased was a spouse, parent, child, or friend, their absence can leave a void that challenges our sense of identity.

The Impact of Loss on Identity

Identity is deeply intertwined with our relationships. When we lose someone significant, we may feel as though a part of ourselves has been lost as well. Grief often involves reconstructing our sense of self as we learn to navigate the world without the person who played a central role in our lives (Neimeyer, 2001).

For example, a widow may struggle with her identity as a wife, while a parent who has lost a child may feel a profound sense of purposelessness. These identity shifts can be disorienting and painful, but they also offer an opportunity for growth and transformation.

Strategies for Navigating Identity Shifts

Acknowledge the Change: Recognize that your identity has shifted and that it is natural to feel uncertain or lost. Allow yourself the space to grieve the person you were while exploring who you are becoming.

Reflect on Your Values: Take time to reflect on your core values and beliefs. What matters most to you? How can you align your life with these values as you move forward?

Explore New Roles and Interests: Consider exploring new roles, hobbies, or interests that align with your evolving identity. This might involve volunteering, pursuing a passion, or joining a community that resonates with you.

Seek Support: Connect with others who have experienced similar losses. Support groups, counseling, or online communities can provide a sense of understanding and validation as you navigate your identity shifts.

Rediscovering Joy

How to Find Meaning in Life Again

In the aftermath of loss, joy can feel elusive or even out of reach. Yet, finding moments of happiness and meaning is an essential part of the healing process. Rediscovering joy does not mean forgetting your loved one; rather, it is a way to honor their memory by embracing life's beauty and potential.

The Role of Meaning-Making in Healing

Finding meaning during grief is often part of the healing process. Viktor Frankl (2006) observed that people who can identify a sense of purpose are better able to endure profound suffering. Meaning-making may emerge through personal growth, helping others, or creating a legacy that honors the person who died.

Some individuals become involved in causes related to their loss. Others turn to creative expression, spiritual reflection, or community service. These pathways can gradually reconnect a grieving person with purpose and hope.

Strategies for Rediscovering Joy

Start Small: Begin by seeking out small moments of joy in your daily life. This might involve savoring a cup of coffee, spending time in nature, or listening to music that uplifts you.

Engage in Acts of Kindness: Helping others can be a powerful way to find meaning and joy. Consider volunteering, mentoring, or simply offering a kind word to someone in need.

Celebrate Your Loved One's Legacy: Find ways to honor their memory with joyful activities. This might involve hosting a celebration of life, creating a memory garden, or participating in an event they would have enjoyed.

Practice Gratitude: Cultivate a daily gratitude practice to shift your focus toward the positive aspects of your life. Write down three things you are grateful for each day, no matter how small.

Story

The First Laugh

For many people, there comes a moment months after a loss when laughter returns unexpectedly.

It may happen during a conversation with a friend, over a shared memory, or in response to something completely ordinary.

The sound can feel surprising, even unsettling. Some people describe an immediate wave of guilt, wondering how laughter could exist in a life that has changed so profoundly.

Yet over time, many discover something important: the moment does not erase grief. It simply makes room for another emotion beside it.

Grief and joy are not opposites. They can exist in the same life at the same time.

The Courage to Start Over

Embracing a New Chapter

Starting over after a loss requires immense courage. It means stepping into the unknown, embracing change, and finding the strength to rebuild your life. While the path forward can be daunting, it also offers an opportunity for growth, resilience, and transformation.

The Challenges of Starting Over

Beginning again often involves navigating practical challenges, such as financial changes, relocation, or adjusting to new routines. It also involves emotional challenges, such as facing fears, overcoming self-doubt, and learning to trust again.

For example, a widow may need to learn new skills to manage household finances, while a parent who has lost a child may struggle to find a sense of purpose in their daily life. These challenges can feel overwhelming, but they also offer an opportunity to build resilience and self-confidence.

Strategies for Embracing a New Chapter

Set Realistic Goals: Break down the process of starting over into manageable steps. Set small, achievable goals that help you move forward, such as learning a new skill or exploring a new hobby.

Embrace Change as an Opportunity: See it as a chance for growth and self-discovery. What new possibilities might this chapter of your life hold? How can you use this time to create a life that aligns with your values and aspirations?

Seek Inspiration: Draw inspiration from others who have rebuilt their lives after loss. Read books, listen to podcasts, or attend workshops that offer guidance and encouragement.

Celebrate Your Progress: Acknowledge and celebrate every step you take, no matter how small. Each step forward is a testament to your courage and resilience.

Exercise: The Beauty of Beginning Again: Rediscovering Life After Loss

Purpose:

This exercise helps you reconnect with life after loss—learning to rebuild without guilt, rediscover joy without shame, and honor your loved one or past life chapter while moving forward.

Step 1: Acknowledging the Empty Space

Before you begin again, you must acknowledge what's no longer there. This step allows you to face the emptiness without judgment.

Prompt:

1. What or who have you lost that changed your daily rhythm?

____

____

2. What feels hardest about beginning again right now?

3. How have you been filling the space that loss left behind, through busyness, silence, withdrawal, or something else?

Reflection:

You can't rebuild on ground you haven't cleared. Honesty is the first act of healing.

Step 2: Permission to Live

Grief often comes with guilt—especially when we start to smile, laugh, or plan again. This exercise helps you release that guilt and reclaim your right to live.

1. What moments of joy have made you feel conflicted or guilty since your loss?

2. If your loved one or your "before" self could speak, what would they want for you now?

3. Write a sentence granting yourself permission to live again.

Example: "It's okay for me to feel joy and still remember."

Reflection:

Healing is not betrayal. It's honoring what was by choosing life.

Step 3: Reconnecting with What Matters

As you begin again, it helps to rediscover what feels meaningful, what sparks curiosity, calm, or connection.

1. What activities, people, or places bring you a sense of peace or energy right now?

2. What values feel most important as you rebuild—compassion, purpose, creativity, service, faith, etc.?

3. How can you make more room for those values in your daily life?

"Sometimes new beginnings don't start with change—they start with remembering what makes you feel alive."

Step 4: Small Steps Forward

Rebuilding doesn't require big moves. Often, it starts with one small, kind decision each day.

Exercise:

List three small actions that help you reconnect with life again—tiny beginnings that feel manageable.

Examples: Taking a morning walk, cooking a meal you love, joining a group, cleaning one space, calling a friend.

"The smallest act of living is still a declaration of hope."

Step 5: Redefining Identity

Loss can leave you wondering who you are now. This step invites you to rediscover yourself—without comparison to who you used to be.

1. Before my loss, I saw myself as

____.

2. Now, I am learning that I am

____.

3. Something new I've discovered about myself is

____.

4. What strengths have emerged that surprise you? (Patience, courage, empathy, independence?)

Reflection:

You are not who you were—and that's okay. Growth after loss is still growth.

Step 6: Honoring What Came Before

Beginning again doesn't mean erasing the past. It means carrying its love forward in a new way.

1. Write one way you will honor what you've lost while still moving forward.

(Example: volunteering, creating art, telling stories, lighting a candle, living kindly.)

2. What lesson or gift did your loss teach you that you now carry with you?

"What you loved deeply will always live within you—it becomes the compass for what comes next."

Step 7: Vision for What's Next

Imagine the next chapter of your life, not as a replacement for what was, but as a continuation of your story.

1. What does "beginning again" look like for you?

2. What would you like this to feel like in the next season of life? Peaceful, purposeful, connected, light?

3. Write one affirmation that will guide you forward:

"I am allowed to start over. My story continues with hope."

Final Reflection

Starting over doesn't mean starting from scratch. It means beginning from experience, strength, and love that loss could not take away.

"Every sunrise is proof that life begins again—no matter what you've been through."

References

Frankl, V. E. (2006). Man's search for meaning. Beacon Press. (Original work published 1946)

Neimeyer, R. A. (2001). Meaning reconstruction and the experience of loss. American Psychological Association.

Chapter 19

When Joy Feels Like Betrayal

Allowing Yourself to Be Happy Again

For many who are grieving, the idea of experiencing joy can feel like a betrayal of their loved one's memory. The guilt of moving on, the fear of forgetting, and the discomfort of laughing again can create a complex emotional landscape. Allowing yourself to feel happiness after loss can be challenging, especially when joy and grief appear to collide.

The Guilt of Moving On

Why Happiness Can Feel Wrong

The guilt of moving on is a common experience for those who are grieving. It often stems from the belief that experiencing joy or happiness means forgetting or dishonoring the person who has died. This guilt can create a barrier to healing, making it difficult to embrace moments of happiness.

The Roots of Guilt in Grief

Guilt in grief often arises from societal expectations, personal beliefs, or unresolved emotions. As Doka (2008) explains, individuals may feel guilty for surviving, for not doing enough to prevent the death, or for finding moments of happiness in the midst of their sorrow.

For example, a parent who has lost a child may feel guilty for laughing or enjoying life, believing that their happiness diminishes the significance of their loss. Similarly, a widow may feel guilty for forming new relationships, fearing that it dishonors their late spouse.

Strategies for Addressing Guilt

Acknowledge Your Feelings: Recognize that guilt is a natural part of the grieving process. Allow yourself to feel and process these emotions without judgment.

Reframe Your Perspective: Reframe your understanding of happiness as a way of honoring your loved one's memory. Consider that they would want you to live a full and joyful life.

Seek Support: Share your feelings of guilt with a trusted friend, family member, or therapist. They can offer perspective and reassurance as you navigate these emotions.

Permission to Laugh

How Joy and Grief Can Coexist

Joy and grief are not mutually exclusive; they can coexist in the same heart. Learning to embrace moments of happiness does not mean letting go of your grief. Instead, it is about finding a balance that allows you to honor your loss while embracing the beauty of life.

The Duality of Joy and Grief

The coexistence of joy and grief is a testament to the complexity of the human experience. As Tedeschi and Calhoun (2004) note, post-traumatic growth often involves finding meaning and joy in the midst of pain. This duality allows individuals to hold space for both their sorrow and their happiness.

For example, you may find yourself laughing at a funny memory of your loved one, only to feel a wave of sadness moments later. These moments of joy and grief are not contradictory; they are a reflection of the depth of your love and connection.

Strategies for Embracing Joy

Give Yourself Permission: Give yourself permission to experience joy without guilt. Remind yourself that happiness does not diminish the significance of your loss.

Create Joyful Rituals: Incorporate joyful activities into your daily life, such as listening to music, spending time with loved ones, or engaging in creative expression.

Practice Mindfulness: Use mindfulness techniques to stay present in moments of joy. Savor the experience without allowing guilt or sadness to overshadow it.

Honoring Their Memory Through Happiness

Living Fully in Their Honor

One of the most powerful ways to honor your loved one's memory is by living a full and joyful life. Embracing happiness does not mean forgetting or moving on; it means carrying their legacy forward in a way that reflects their love and impact.

The Concept of Living in Honor

Living in honor of your loved one involves finding ways to celebrate their life and values through your actions and choices. As Neimeyer (2012) observes, this can create a sense of continuity and connection, even in their absence.

For example, you might honor your loved one by pursuing a passion they encouraged, helping others in their name, or simply living with the kindness and compassion they embodied.

Strategies for Honoring Their Memory Through Happiness

Create a Legacy of Joy: Find ways to infuse joy into your life in honor of your loved one. This might involve participating in activities they enjoyed, sharing their favorite stories, or creating a tradition that celebrates their spirit.

Live Their Values: Reflect on the values and principles that were important to your loved one. How can you incorporate these values into your own life as a way of honoring their memory?

Share Their Story: Share your loved one's story with others, keeping their memory alive through your words and actions. This can create a sense of connection and continuity, even as you embrace new joys.

Exercise: When Love Changes Shape

Purpose:

This brief exercise helps you explore how love continues even after loss—how it changes form, but not presence.

Step 1: Remembering with Warmth

Think of one moment that still makes you smile when you remember your loved one or what you lost.

Prompt:

What was happening in that moment?

What feeling does it bring up for you now?

"Love doesn't disappear; it shifts from something you hold to something that holds you."

Step 2: Love in New Form

Love may return through small signs—memories, coincidences, habits, or kindnesses you carry on.

Prompt:

Where do you still feel their presence or influence today?

What's one way you can continue their legacy or honor what you shared?

Step 3: Affirmation of Connection

Write a short sentence that captures how love now lives within you.

Example:

"Our love didn't end; it simply found a new way to be."

Your version:

Reflection:

Even goodbyes can become bridges. Love doesn't vanish—it evolves.

References

Doka, K. J. (2008). *Disenfranchised grief: New directions, challenges, and strategies for practice.* Research Press.

Neimeyer, R. A. (2012). Techniques of grief therapy: Creative practices for counseling the bereaved. Routledge.

Tedeschi, R. G., & Calhoun, L. G. (2004). Posttraumatic growth: Conceptual foundations and empirical evidence. Psychological Inquiry, 15(1), 1-18

Chapter 20

Honoring Their Legacy

Keeping Their Memory Alive in Meaningful Ways

Grief does not end with the passage of time; instead, it evolves into a lasting relationship with memory and love. Honoring the legacy of a loved one is a powerful way to keep their spirit alive, transforming grief into a source of meaning and connection. This chapter explores the many ways to honor a loved one's memory, from acts of remembrance and storytelling to living the values and passions that mattered to them.

Acts of Remembrance

Charity, Tributes, and Other Ways to Honor Them

Acts of remembrance are tangible expressions of love and respect for the person who has died. These acts can take many forms, from charitable donations to personal tributes, and they serve as a way to keep their memory alive while contributing to the world in their name.

The Role of Acts of Remembrance in Healing

Acts of remembrance provide a renewed purpose and continuity in the face of loss. Creating meaningful rituals and tributes can help individuals integrate their loss into their ongoing life narrative, fostering a sense of connection and healing (Neimeyer, 2012).

For example, establishing a scholarship fund in your loved one's name or volunteering for a cause they cared about can create a lasting legacy that reflects their values and passions. These acts not only honor their memory but also provide a sense of meaning and fulfillment for the bereaved.

Examples of Acts of Remembrance

Charitable Contributions: Donate to a charity or organization that was meaningful to your loved one. This could be a cause they supported, such as cancer research, animal welfare, or education.

Memorial Events: Organize an annual event, such as a walk, run, or fundraiser, to honor your loved one's memory. These events can bring together friends, family, and community members to celebrate their life and impact.

Personal Tributes: Create a personal tribute, such as a memory garden, a piece of art, or a scrapbook. These tangible expressions of love can serve as a source of comfort and connection.

Legacy Projects: Start a project that reflects your loved one's passions and values. This might involve writing a book, creating a documentary, or launching a community initiative in their honor.

Sharing Their Story

How to Keep Their Spirit Alive Through Storytelling

Storytelling is one of the most powerful ways to keep a loved one's memory alive. By sharing their story, you invite others to participate in the ongoing narrative of their life, ensuring that their spirit continues to inspire and connect.

The Healing Power of Storytelling

Storytelling allows us to make sense of our experiences, process emotions, and create meaning (Pennebaker & Seagal, 1999). In the context of grief, sharing stories about a loved one can help you feel closer to them and provide growing comfort and validation.

For example, recounting a funny anecdote or a cherished moment can bring a sense of joy and connection, even in the midst of sadness. It also allows others to see your loved one through your eyes, fostering a deeper understanding of their impact on your life.

How to Share Their Story Effectively

Create a Memory Book or Journal: Compile photos, letters, and stories in a memory book or journal. This can serve as a tangible keepsake that you can revisit and share with others. Encourage family and friends to contribute their own memories, creating a collective tribute to your loved one.

Host a Memory-Sharing Gathering: Organize a gathering where friends and family can come together to share stories and memories. This could be a formal event, such as a memorial service, or an informal gathering, such as a dinner or picnic. The act of coming together to remember can be deeply healing.

Use Technology to Preserve Memories: In today's digital age, there are countless ways to preserve and share memories online. Create a memorial website, a social media page, or a video tribute that others can access. These platforms allow you to reach a wider audience and create a lasting legacy.

Living Their Values

Incorporating Their Beliefs and Passions into Your Life

One of the most profound ways to honor a loved one's legacy is by living their values and passions. By incorporating their beliefs and principles into your own life, you create a living tribute that reflects their impact and influence.

The Concept of Continuing Bonds

The concept of *continuing bonds* emphasizes that relationships with loved ones do not simply end with death; they evolve into new forms of connection (Klass, Silverman, & Nickman, 1996). Living according to their values can be a meaningful way to maintain that connection.

For example, if your loved one cared deeply about environmental conservation, you might adopt sustainable practices or volunteer with conservation groups. If they valued kindness and compassion, you might consciously practice those qualities in everyday life.

Strategies for Living Their Values

Reflect on Their Beliefs: Take time to reflect on the values and principles that were important to your loved one. How can you incorporate these beliefs into your own life?

Set Intentional Goals: Set goals that align with your loved one's passions and values. This might involve pursuing a cause they cared about, learning a new skill, or making a positive impact in their community.

Pass On Their Wisdom: Share the lessons and wisdom your loved one imparted to you with others. Whether it's through storytelling, mentoring, or teaching, passing on their knowledge ensures that their influence continues to grow.

Celebrate Their Life: Find ways to celebrate your loved one's life and the joy they brought to others. This could be through an annual event, a creative project, or simply by living a life that reflects their spirit.

EXERCISE: LEGACY IN ACTION

Legacy-in-Action (15 Minutes)

Purpose: Turn love into action by choosing one simple way to honor their memory today.

Time: 10–15 minutes

Materials: One sheet of paper or notes app; optional timer

Steps

1. Ground (1 minute): Take 4 slow breaths. Place a hand on your chest; name one value they lived (e.g., kindness, courage, curiosity).

2. Three Paths (3 minutes): Draw three short headings and jot 2–3 ideas under each:

Act of Remembrance (donation, small tribute, photo on the table, a candle)

Story to Share (a moment, a lesson, a funny line)

Value to Live (one behavior that reflects them today)

3. Pick-One Rule (2 minutes): Circle one low-effort item that feels doable today (≤10 minutes).

4. Micro-Plan (3 minutes): Write a one-line plan with a time stamp.

Example: "At 7:30 pm, text my sister the story about our beach trip."

If choosing a value, make it behavioral: "Hold the door for three people," "Email a thank-you."

5. Do It (3–5 minutes): Follow through once. Keep it small and complete.

Reflect (2–3 minutes)

What emotion rose up as you acted?

If they could see that moment, what might they say?

What tiny version of this could you repeat weekly?

Trauma-informed tips: You can stop at any point. If emotions surge, return to breath and name 5 things you see. Choose the easiest option—consistency matters more than intensity.

References

Klass, D., Silverman, P. R., & Nickman, S. L. (Eds.). (1996). Continuing bonds: New understandings of grief. Taylor & Francis.

Neimeyer, R. A. (2012). Techniques of grief therapy: Creative practices for counseling the bereaved. Routledge.

Pennebaker, J. W., & Seagal, J. D. (1999). Forming a story: The health benefits of narrative. Journal of Clinical Psychology, 55(10), 1243–1254.

Chapter 21

Grief and Growth

How Loss Changes Us and Helps Us Grow

Grief is often described as a transformative experience, one that reshapes our lives in profound and unexpected ways. While the pain of loss can feel overwhelming, it can also be a catalyst for growth, resilience, and self-discovery. Growth after loss does not erase suffering, but it can reshape the way we live.

The Transformative Power of Grief

How Loss Reshapes Us

Grief has the power to change us in ways we never imagined. It forces us to confront the fragility of life, reevaluate our priorities, and find new meaning in our experiences. Transformation is often referred to as post-traumatic growth (Tedeschi & Calhoun, 2004).

The Process of Post-Traumatic Growth

Post-traumatic growth involves finding meaning and purpose in the midst of suffering. It is not about erasing the pain of loss but about integrating that pain into a new understanding of life. Neimeyer (2001) reports that this transformation often involves a shift in perspective, where individuals develop a deeper appreciation for life, stronger relationships, and a greater sense of personal strength.

For example, someone who has lost a loved one may develop a greater sense of empathy and compassion, using their experience to help others who are grieving. Others may find new passions or pursue long-held dreams after recognizing how fragile and precious life can be.

Strategies for Embracing Transformation

Reflect on Your Growth: Take time to consider how grief has changed you. What have you learned about yourself? How have your priorities and values shifted?

Find Meaning in Your Loss: Explore ways to find meaning in your loss, whether through helping others, pursuing a passion, or creating a legacy in honor of your loved one.

Embrace Change: View change as an opportunity for growth and self-discovery. What new possibilities might emerge in the life you are now rebuilding?

Finding Strength in Vulnerability

Embracing Your New Self

Grief often leaves us feeling vulnerable and exposed, yet it is in this vulnerability that we find our greatest strength. Embracing your new self, with all its complexities and contradictions, is an essential part of the healing process.

The Role of Vulnerability in Grief

Grief often leaves us feeling vulnerable, yet that vulnerability can open the door to healing. Brown (2012) explains that vulnerability allows us to connect with others, process our emotions, and ultimately find healing. Through vulnerability, we discover our resilience and capacity for growth.

For example, sharing your grief with others can create a sense of connection and understanding, even in the midst of pain. Allowing yourself to be vulnerable also opens the door to self-compassion, as you learn to treat yourself with kindness and patience.

Strategies for Embracing Vulnerability

Share Your Story: Share your grief journey with others, whether through writing, speaking, or participating in support groups. This can help you feel less alone and more connected.

Practice Self-Compassion: Be kind and patient with yourself as you navigate grief. Recognize that healing is a gradual process and that it's okay to have difficult days.

Seek Support: Surround yourself with individuals who uplift and support you. A strong support network can provide encouragement and help you navigate difficult emotions.

Grief and Relationships

How Loss Influences Families and Communities

Grief rarely affects only one person. It ripples out to affect our relationships, families, and communities. Understanding the broader impact of loss can help us navigate its complexities and find ways to support one another.

The Impact of Grief on Relationships

Grief can strain relationships as individuals struggle with their own emotions and ways of coping. For example, a couple who has lost a child may struggle to communicate their grief, leading to feelings of isolation and misunderstanding. Similarly, friends and family members may feel unsure of how to offer support, creating a sense of distance.

At the same time, grief can also strengthen relationships, as individuals come together to support one another and share their experiences. As Stroebe, Schut, and Stroebe (2007) note, grieving together can create a sense of solidarity and connection.

The Role of Community in Grief

Community plays a vital role after a loss, offering a network of support, understanding, and shared connection. Whether through formal support groups, religious communities, or informal networks of friends and family, community can offer a sense of belonging and validation.

For example, a community that comes together to honor a loved one's memory can create a powerful sense of connection and continuity. Similarly, participating in community events or initiatives can provide a sense of purpose and meaning in the midst of grief.

Strategies for Navigating the Influence of Loss

Communicate Openly: Share your grief and needs with those around you. Let them know how they can support you and be willing to listen to their experiences as well.

Foster Connection: Look for ways to connect with others who have experienced loss. This might involve joining a support group, attending community events, or simply reaching out to a friend.

Create a Supportive Environment: Foster empathy, understanding, and open communication for yourself and others. This can help strengthen relationships and create a sense of community in the face of loss.

EXERCISE: PERMISSION TO FEEL JOY

Permission to Feel Joy (12–15 Minutes)

Purpose: Practice experiencing moments of joy or relief without guilt as you continue healing.

Time: 12–15 minutes

Materials: Paper or notes app; optional timer

Steps

1. Arrive (1 minute): 4 slow breaths. Name one sensation you feel (e.g., "warm hands," "tight chest") to anchor in the present.

2. Name the Pull (2 minutes): Write one sentence that captures the inner conflict:

"When I feel happy, a voice says I'm forgetting them."

3. Reframe (2 minutes): Write a compassionate counter-sentence as if your loved one spoke to you:

"Your smile honors me—you're not leaving me behind."

4. Tiny Joy (3–5 minutes): Choose one small, low-effort joy (≤5 minutes): step outside and feel the sun, play 30 seconds of a favorite song, sip tea mindfully, stretch your shoulders. Do it now.

5. Guilt Companion Script (1 minute): If guilt appears, whisper:

"Both/and: I can miss you and feel this moment of light."

6. Commit (1 minute): Schedule one repeat for tomorrow (same tiny joy, same time). Add a reminder titled "Joy is allowed."

Reflect (2–3 minutes)

What did the guilt-voice say? What did your compassionate voice say back?

Where did the joy land in your body (lightness, warmth, ease)?

One sentence you'll keep for the week: "I'm allowed to feel ___ and still love ___."

Trauma-informed tips: You can stop anytime. Keep the joy tiny to avoid overwhelming. If activation spikes, orient to the room (name 5 things you see, 4 you feel, 3 you hear).

References

Brown, B. (2012). Daring greatly: How the courage to be vulnerable transforms the way we live, love, parent, and lead. Gotham Books.

Klass, D., Silverman, P. R., & Nickman, S. L. (1996). Continuing bonds: New understandings of grief. Taylor & Francis.

Neimeyer, R. A. (2001). Meaning reconstruction and the experience of loss. American Psychological Association.

Pennebaker, J. W., & Seagal, J. D. (1999). Forming a story: The health benefits of narrative. Journal of Clinical Psychology, 55(10), 1243-1254

Stroebe, M., Schut, H., & Stroebe, W. (2007). Health outcomes of bereavement. The Lancet, 370(9603), 1960-1973.

Tedeschi, R. G., & Calhoun, L. G. (2004). Posttraumatic growth: Conceptual foundations and empirical evidence. Psychological Inquiry, 15(1), 1-18.

Chapter 22

The Role of Forgiveness in Healing

Letting Go of Guilt, Regret, and Anger

Forgiveness is a powerful yet often misunderstood aspect of the grieving process. It is not about condoning hurtful actions or forgetting the pain of loss; rather, it is about releasing the emotional burdens of guilt, regret, and anger that can hinder healing. Forgiveness plays a transformative role in grief, focusing on forgiving oneself, forgiving others, and the freedom that forgiveness brings.

Forgiving Yourself

Releasing Guilt Over Things Said or Unsaid

Guilt is a common and often paralyzing emotion in grief. It can stem from regrets about things said or unsaid, actions taken or not taken, or perceived failures in the relationship with the deceased. Forgiving yourself is a critical step in the healing process, allowing you to move forward with compassion and self-acceptance.

The Weight of Guilt in Grief

Guilt during grief often emerges from the belief that we could have or should have done more to prevent the loss or ease the suffering of our loved one. As Doka (2008) explains, this "if only" thinking can trap individuals in a cycle of self-blame and rumination, preventing them from fully processing their grief.

For example, a caregiver may feel guilty for not being able to save their loved one, while a family member may regret not expressing their love or resolving a conflict before it was too late. These feelings of guilt can be overwhelming, but they are a common response to loss.

A Letter Never Sent

Story

Months after her brother's death, Elena found herself dwelling on words she had never spoken. Their relationship had been close, yet like many siblings, they had occasionally argued and drifted apart during busy periods of life.

One evening, she sat down with a notebook and began writing a letter to him. At first, the words came slowly. She wrote about childhood memories, the things she admired in him, and the regrets she had carried since his passing.

The letter was never meant to be mailed. It was simply a space where she could speak openly without interruption or judgment.

When she finished, Elena folded the pages and placed them inside a small box that held photographs of her brother.

Writing the letter did not erase the sadness she felt, but it gave voice to emotions that had been difficult to express. In putting those thoughts on paper, she felt a small sense of peace—an acknowledgment of the bond that still remained.

Practicing Self-Forgiveness

Acknowledge Your Feelings: Allow yourself to recognize feelings of guilt without judgment. These emotions often reflect the depth of your care for the person who died.

Challenge Unrealistic Expectations: Reflect on whether your guilt stems from realistic or unrealistic expectations. Could you truly have controlled the outcome? Often, we did the best we could with the knowledge and resources available at the time.

Practice Self-Compassion: Treat yourself with the same kindness and understanding you would offer a friend. Being human includes making imperfect choices.

Seek Support: Share your feelings of guilt with a trusted friend, family member, or therapist. They can offer perspective and reassurance, helping you release the burden of self-blame.

Forgiving Others

Letting Go of Resentment and Blame

Grief can sometimes be accompanied by feelings of anger and resentment, particularly if the loss was sudden, traumatic, or involved unresolved conflicts. Forgiving others does not mean excusing their actions; rather, it means releasing the hold that anger and blame have on your heart, allowing you to find peace and move forward.

The Role of Anger in Grief

Anger is a natural and often necessary emotion in grief. It can arise from feelings of injustice, helplessness, or betrayal, and it can be directed at oneself, others, or even the deceased. Kübler-Ross and Kessler (2005) describe anger as one of the emotional responses that can appear during grief and, when processed in healthy ways, may lead to greater understanding and acceptance.

However, when anger remains unresolved, it can hinder healing and create barriers in relationships. Forgiving others is a way of breaking free from this cycle, allowing you to focus on the love and connection that remain.

Strategies for Forgiving Others

Acknowledge Your Anger: Recognize and validate your feelings of anger without judgment. Understand that these emotions are a natural response to loss and pain.

Reflect on the Source of Anger: Consider the root cause of your anger. Is it directed at a specific person, a situation, or the circumstances of the loss? Understanding the source of your anger can help you address it more effectively.

Practice Empathy: Try to see the situation from the other person's perspective. This does not mean excusing their actions but rather understanding the context and motivations behind them.

Release the Hold of Anger: Letting go of anger does not happen overnight. It is a gradual process that involves consciously choosing to release resentment and focus on healing. Techniques such as journaling, meditation, or therapy can support release and healing.

The Freedom of Forgiveness

How It Opens the Door to Healing

Forgiveness, whether of oneself or others, is a liberating act that opens the door to healing and growth. It allows you to release the emotional burdens of guilt, regret, and anger, creating space for love, compassion, and peace.

The Transformative Power of Forgiveness

Forgiveness is not about forgetting or condoning. Instead, it involves freeing oneself from the emotional weight of resentment. Research on forgiveness suggests that it often involves a shift in perspective, allowing individuals to release negative emotions and focus more fully on the positive aspects of their lives and relationships (Worthington, 2005). For example, forgiving yourself for past mistakes can help you embrace self-compassion and self-acceptance, while forgiving others can restore a sense of connection and understanding. These acts of forgiveness create a foundation for healing and growth.

Strategies for Embracing Forgiveness

Set an Intention to Forgive: Make a conscious decision to forgive, recognizing that it is a process rather than a single event. Set an intention to release negative emotions and focus on healing.

Practice Gratitude: Cultivate a daily gratitude practice to shift your focus toward the positive aspects of your life. This can help you develop a more compassionate and forgiving mindset.

Seek Closure: Engage in activities that help you find closure, such as writing a letter, creating a ritual, or having a conversation with the person you are forgiving. These acts can provide a sense of resolution and peace.

Celebrate Your Progress: Acknowledge and celebrate the progress you make in your forgiveness journey. Each step forward is a testament to your strength and resilience.

EXERCISE: RE-ENTERING LIFE

The 5% Shift: Gentle Reentry into Life (12–15 Minutes)

Purpose: Identify one small, value-aligned step that nudges you back into life without overwhelm.

Time: 12–15 minutes

Materials: Paper or notes app; optional timer

Steps

1. Settle (1 minute): 4 slow breaths. Name one word for how you feel right now.

2. Choose a Value (2 minutes): Write one value you want more of this month (e.g., connection, creativity, health, service).

3. Brainstorm Tiny Steps (3 minutes): List 5 actions that express that value in ≤10 minutes each.

Examples: text a check-in to one person; sketch for 7 minutes; walk to the end of the block; donate $5; water a plant in their honor.

4. Pick the 5% Shift (2 minutes): Circle the easiest option—the one that feels like a 5% effort upgrade, not a total overhaul.

5. Make It Real (2 minutes): Write a one-line plan with a time and place.

"At 6:40 pm, I'll take a 7-minute walk and notice three trees."

6. Do It (2–5 minutes): Follow through once, gently.

Reflect (2 minutes)

What made this step feel doable?

Where did you notice ease or resistance in your body?

One sentence to carry forward: "Small still counts."

Trauma-informed tips: Stop anytime. If activation rises, orient to the room (5 things you see, 4 you feel, 3 you hear). Choose steps that are small, repeatable, and optional.

References

Doka, K. J. (2008). Disenfranchised grief: Recognizing hidden sorrow. Lexington Books.

Kübler-Ross, E., & Kessler, D. (2005). On grief and grieving: Finding the meaning of grief through the five stages of loss. Scribner.

Worthington, E. L. (2005). Handbook of forgiveness. Routledge.

Chapter 23

The Ripple Effect of Loss

How Grief Impacts Relationships and Community

Grief is not an isolated experience; it ripples out to affect our relationships, families, and communities. Understanding the broader impact of loss can help us navigate its complexities and find ways to support one another. Loss can strengthen bonds, navigate changed relationships, and build a supportive community. In earlier chapters we explored how grief transforms us internally. Loss also extends outward, influencing our relationships, families, and communities in powerful ways.

Strengthening Bonds

How Loss Can Bring People Closer

While grief can strain relationships, it can also bring people closer together. Shared experiences of loss often foster deeper empathy and understanding among those who mourn together.

The Role of Shared Grief

Shared grief can create a powerful sense of connection, as individuals come together to support one another and honor the memory of the person who died. As Stroebe, Schut, and Stroebe (2007) note, mourning together can strengthen social bonds and reinforce community.

For example, a family that comes together to plan a memorial service or share stories about their loved one may find that their relationships are deepened and strengthened. Similarly, friends who support one another through grief may develop a deeper sense of trust and understanding.

Strategies for Strengthening Bonds

Communicate Openly: Share your feelings and experiences with those around you. Open communication can foster understanding and connection, even in the midst of pain.

Create Shared Rituals: Engage in rituals or activities that honor the memory of your loved one. This might involve hosting a memorial event, creating a memory book, or participating in a community project.

Offer and Accept Support: Be willing to offer support to others who are grieving, and accept support when it is offered to you. This mutual exchange can create a sense of solidarity and connection.

Navigating Changed Relationships

When Grief Alters Friendships or Family Dynamics

Grief can alter the dynamics of relationships, creating new challenges and opportunities for growth. Friendships may shift, family roles may change, and new boundaries may need to be established.

The Impact of Grief on Relationships

Grief can strain relationships, as individuals cope with loss in different ways. For example, siblings who have lost a parent may grieve very differently—one wanting to talk frequently about memories while another prefers silence or distraction. These differences can create misunderstandings or feelings of distance. Similarly, friends and extended family members may feel unsure how to offer support, which can unintentionally deepen feelings of isolation.

At the same time, grief can also create opportunities for growth and transformation. Working through grief together can lead to greater understanding, empathy, and connection (Neimeyer, 2012).

Strategies for Navigating Changed Relationships

Communicate Your Needs: Clearly communicate your needs and boundaries to those around you. Let them know how they can support you and be willing to listen to their experiences as well.

Be Patient and Understanding: Recognize that everyone grieves differently and that relationships may shift as a result. Be patient and understanding as you navigate these changes.

Seek Mediation if Needed: If conflicts arise, consider seeking the help of a mediator or therapist to facilitate communication and resolution.

Building a Supportive Community

Creating a Network of Care and Understanding

After a loss, people often discover that grief reaches far beyond the individual. Families, friends, and communities are touched as well.. Whether through formal support groups, religious communities, or informal networks of friends and family, community can provide belonging and validation.

For some individuals, structured grief support groups provide a particularly meaningful form of connection. Sitting with others who have experienced similar losses can ease the isolation that often accompanies grief. Many communities now offer groups designed for specific life stages, including young adults navigating the loss of a parent or close family member. Hearing how others face similar milestones, careers, relationships, and life transitions, can help people realize they are not alone in the complexity of their grief.

The Role of Community in Grief

Community provides a sense of connection and continuity in the face of loss. As Klass, Silverman, and Nickman (1996) suggest, the concept of "continuing bonds" emphasizes the ongoing relationship between the bereaved and the person who has died, even after death. Community can help maintain these bonds, providing a sense of support and understanding.

For example, a community that comes together to honor a loved one’s memory can create a powerful sense of connection and continuity. Similarly, participating in community events or initiatives can provide a sense of purpose and meaning during times of grief.

Strategies for Building a Supportive Community

Join Support Groups: Consider joining a grief support group, either in-person or online. These groups provide a safe space to share your experiences and connect with others who understand your pain.

Participate in Community Events: Engage in community events or initiatives honoring your loved one's memory. This might involve volunteering, organizing a fundraiser, or participating in a memorial event.

Foster Empathy and Understanding: Create a supportive environment for yourself and others by fostering empathy, understanding, and open communication. This can help strengthen relationships and create a close community in the face of loss.

EXERCISE: IDENTITY

Identity Map: Then / Now / Becoming (12–15 Minutes)

Purpose: Gently explore who you are after loss and name one small step toward the life you're becoming.

Time: 12–15 minutes

Materials: Paper or notes app; pen; optional timer

Steps

1. Arrive (1 minute): 4 slow breaths. Feel your feet on the floor; notice one sound in the room.

2. Three Circles (2 minutes): Draw three headings down the page: Then, Now, Becoming.

3. Then (2 minutes): List 3–5 roles/qualities you identified with before the loss (e.g., "planner," "Saturday breakfast buddy," "runner").

4. Now (3 minutes): List 3–5 truths about you today—both strengths and struggles (e.g., "tired but present," "more patient," "avoids crowds," "showing up for family").

5. Becoming (3 minutes): Imagine a compassionate future self. List 3 small qualities or practices you want to grow (e.g., "ask for help once a week," "create a quiet morning ritual," "say no without apology").

6. One Bridge Step (1–2 minutes): Choose one tiny action you can do in ≤10 minutes this week that moves you from Now toward Becoming. Write a one-line plan with date/time.

Example: "Wednesday 7:15 pm—text Maya to walk two blocks with me."

Reflect (2–3 minutes)

Which word from Now felt most honest?

Which Becoming item felt energizing (not overwhelming)?

Finish this sentence: "Even in grief, I am someone who ___."

Trauma-informed tips: You can stop anytime. If activation rises, look around and name 5 things you see, 4 you feel, 3 you hear. Keep the bridge step very small and optional.

References

Klass, D., Silverman, P. R., & Nickman, S. L. (Eds.). (1996). Continuing bonds: New understandings of grief. Taylor & Francis.

Neimeyer, R. A. (2012). Techniques of grief therapy: Creative practices for counseling the bereaved. Routledge.

Stroebe, M., Schut, H., & Stroebe, W. (2007). Health outcomes of bereavement. The Lancet, 370(9603), 1960–1973.

Chapter 24

A Letter to the Departed

A Final Reflection, Closure, and Love

Writing a letter to a departed loved one can be a powerful and healing act. It allows you to express your emotions, reflect on your relationship, and find a sense of closure. This chapter explores the healing power of writing, what to say when they're gone, and how a letter can bring peace.

The Healing Power of Writing

Why Putting Pen to Paper Helps

Writing is a therapeutic tool that can help you process emotions, gain clarity, find meaning in your experiences, and give voice to grief that may otherwise remain unspoken. Expressive writing can reduce stress, improve emotional well-being, and foster a sense of closure (Pennebaker & Seagal, 1999).

The Benefits of Writing in Grief

Writing allows you to externalize your emotions, creating a tangible expression of your inner experience. This can be particularly healing in the context of grief, where emotions can feel overwhelming and difficult to articulate.

For example, writing a letter to a departed loved one can help you express feelings of love, regret, and gratitude that may have been left unsaid. It can also provide a sense of connection and continuity, allowing you to maintain a bond with the deceased.

Strategies for Using Writing as a Healing Tool

Set Aside Time to Write: Dedicate a specific time and place for writing, free from distractions. This can help you create a quiet peace through ritual and intentionality.

Write Freely and Honestly: Allow yourself to write freely and honestly, without worrying about grammar or structure. The goal is to express your emotions, not to create a perfect piece of writing.

Reflect on Your Writing: After writing, take time to reflect on your words and the emotions they evoke. This can help you gain insight and clarity into your grief journey.

What to Say When They're Gone

Expressing Love, Regret, and Gratitude

A letter to a departed loved one can include a range of emotions and reflections. It is an opportunity to express your love, acknowledge regrets, and offer gratitude for the time you shared.

Expressing Love

Begin by expressing your love and appreciation for the person who has died. Share specific memories or qualities you cherish and let them know how much they meant to you.

Acknowledging Regrets

If there are unresolved conflicts or regrets, acknowledge them in your letter. This is not about assigning blame but about expressing your feelings and seeking closure.

Offering Gratitude

Express gratitude for the time you shared and the impact they had on your life. Let them know how they have shaped you and how you will carry their memory forward.

Finding Closure Through Words

How a Letter Can Bring Peace

Writing a letter to a departed loved one can provide a feeling of closure, allowing you to release unresolved emotions and find peace. It is a way to honor their memory and maintain a connection, even in their absence.

The Role of Closure in Grief

Closure does not mean forgetting or leaving the past behind. Instead, it involves finding peace and resolution while learning how to carry the loss forward in a meaningful way. Neimeyer (2012) noted that closure often includes integrating the loss into the story of one's life, finding ways to maintain a continuing bond with the person who died, allowing memories to coexist with the present, and gradually restoring peace and continuity.

For example, writing a letter can help you process unresolved emotions, express your love and gratitude, and find a sense of closure. It is a way to honor your relationship and maintain a bond with the loved one who passed away.

Strategies for Finding Closure Through Writing

Write from the Heart: Allow yourself to write freely and honestly, expressing your emotions without judgment or censorship.

Create a Ritual: After writing, create a ritual to honor your letter. This might involve reading it aloud, burning it, or placing it in a special location.

Reflect on Your Journey: Take time to reflect on your grief journey and the progress you have made. Recognize that closure is a gradual process and that each step forward is a testament to your strength and resilience.

Exercise: Ripple Map

Purpose: turn a meaningful memory into one small action you can take this week.

Time: 15–20 minutes to plan, 10 minutes to act.

Materials: paper or notebook, pen.

Steps:

1. Write one sentence that captures a moment or quality you miss about your loved one.

2. Draw a small circle on the page and put that sentence inside it.

3. Around the circle, add three "ripples" and label them:

What I can do today

Who I can include

How I will feel afterward

4. In each ripple, list 2–3 concrete ideas. Keep them small. Example: share a story with a friend, cook their favorite side dish, donate $5 to a cause they cared about, send a thank-you text to someone they once helped.

5. Pick one idea from the "today" ripple and schedule it. Put the exact time in your calendar.

Reflect:

What changed in your mood before and after the action?

Did this feel like honoring, not performing?

What would you try next time?

Optional add-on: take one photo that represents your action and save it in a "Ripples" album to look back on during hard days.

References

Neimeyer, R. A. (2012). Techniques of grief therapy: Creative practices for counseling the bereaved. Routledge.

Pennebaker, J. W., & Seagal, J. D. (1999). Forming a story: The health benefits of narrative. Journal of Clinical Psychology, 55(10), 1243-1254

Conclusion: Carrying Love Forward

Grief is not a journey with a clear endpoint. It does not lead to a place where pain disappears, and life returns to what it once was. Instead, grief becomes part of the story we continue to live, reflecting the depth of the love we carry for those who are no longer physically with us.

Over time, many people discover that grief cannot be rushed or resolved. It is something we gradually learn to live with, integrating loss into our lives as we continue to move forward. In the process, grief often reveals what matters most: love, connection, and the preciousness of life itself.

Carrying love forward means honoring the people we have lost through the lives we continue to build. Their influence remains present in our memories, our values, and the stories we share. In this way, the bonds we formed do not end; they change form.

The journey of grief will continue beyond the pages of this book. There will be moments when loss feels close again and others when life brings unexpected peace. Moving forward does not mean leaving our loved ones behind. It means carrying them with us while allowing ourselves to keep living.

If this book has offered you comfort, understanding, or companionship along the way, then it has served its purpose.

Love remains.
And it continues to guide us forward.

With compassion,

Sheila Mallett-Smith
Jiles Smith II

www.ingramcontent.com/pod-product-compliance
Lightning Source LLC
LaVergne TN
LVHW010649110826
845149LV00014B/3005

* 9 7 8 1 9 6 7 0 5 5 2 1 0 *